Buffalo Bill Cody

Legends of the Wild West

Sitting Bull

Billy the Kid

Calamity Jane

Buffalo Bill Cody

Crazy Horse

Davy Crockett

Wyatt Earp

Geronimo

Wild Bill Hickok

Jesse James

Nat Love

Annie Oakley

Buffalo Bill Cody

Ronald A. Reis

CHELSEA HOUSE
PUBLISHERS
An imprint of Infobase Publishing

Buffalo Bill Cody

Copyright © 2010 by Infobase Publishing

Chelsea House
An imprint of Infobase Publishing
132 West 31st Street
New York NY 10001

Library of Congress Cataloging-in-Publication Data
Reis, Ronald A.
  Buffalo Bill Cody / Ronald A. Reis.
    p. cm. — (Legends of the Wild West)
  Includes bibliographical references and index.
  ISBN 978-1-60413-528-2 (hardcover : alk. paper) 1. Buffalo Bill,
1846-1917—Juvenile literature. 2. Pioneers—West (U.S.)—Biography--Juvenile
literature. 3. Frontier and pioneer life--West (U.S.)--Juvenile literature. 4.
Entertainers—United States—Biography—Juvenile literature. 5. Buffalo Bill's Wild
West Show—Juvenile literature. 6. West (U.S.)—Biography—Juvenile literature. I.
Title. II. Series.
  F594.B94R45 2010
  978'.02092—dc22
  [B]   2010006592

Chelsea House books are available at special discounts when purchased in bulk quantities for businesses, associations, institutions, or sales promotions. Please call our Special Sales Department in New York at (212) 967-8800 or (800) 322-8755.

You can find Chelsea House on the World Wide Web at
http://www.chelseahouse.com.

Text design by Kerry Casey
Cover design by Keith Trego
Composition by EJB Publishing Services
Cover printed by Bang Printing, Brainerd, Minn.
Book printed and bound by Bang Printing, Brainerd, Minn.
Date printed: August 2010
Printed in the United States of America

10 9 8 7 6 5 4 3 2 1

CONTENTS

1 Centaur of the Prairie 7

2 Boy Plainsman 17

3 Buffalo Bill 28

4 Chief of Scouts 39

5 On Stage 50

6 Showman Extraordinaire 60

7 Crowned Heads of Europe 71

8 American Indians and the Wild West 83

9 Congress of Rough Riders 93

10 Farewell the Wild West 105

Chronology 116

Timeline 116

Glossary 119

Bibliography 121

Further Resources 126

Picture Credits 128

Index 129

About the Author 133

CENTAUR
OF THE PRAIRIE

An advertisement in the California newspaper, in the want ads, made it clear as to what type of young men were needed to make the runs. "Wanted," declared the 1860 bulletin. "Young, skinny, wiry fellows. Not over 18. Must be expert riders. Willing to risk death daily. Orphans preferred."

William Frederick Cody of Leavenworth, Kansas, seemed to fit the bill. At 14 years of age, he was certainly young enough. Having traveled clear to Denver and back in his job as a wagon train message carrier, he definitely knew how to ride. Moreover, young Will was, like most boys of the midwestern Plains, no stranger to risk and adversity. True, he was not, strictly speaking, an orphan, though his dad had died of complications from a stab wound in 1857. No matter, most riders for the Pony Express were not orphans.

Though Cody claimed to have ridden for the Pony Express on a previous occasion, it was in the summer of 1860 that he was, it would seem, hired for an extended period. Joseph A. Slade, the notorious desperado in charge of the division from Julesburg to Rocky Ridge, with headquarters at Horse Station, offered the boy work. According to Cody in his 1879 autobiography, *The Life of Buffalo*

Bill, the following exchange took place between the two when Will asked for a job:

> "My boy, you are too young for a pony express rider. It takes men for that business."
>
> "I rode two months last year on Bill Trotter's division, sir, and filled the bill then; and I think I am better able to ride now," said I.
>
> "What! Are you the boy that was riding there, and was called the youngest rider on the road?"
>
> "I am the same boy," I replied, confident that everything was now all right for me.
>
> "I have heard of you before. You are a year or so older now, and I think you can stand it. I'll give you a trial anyhow and if you weaken you can come back to Horseshoe Station and tend stock."

It would appear that Will had, quick enough, latched on to a young plainsman's dream job, riding for the daring Pony Express—and this at an age when many adolescents were hunched over a desk, studying in school.

RECORD RIDE?

The Pony Express was the brainchild of Russell, Majors, and Waddell; however, not all of the partners of what became a subsidiary of the firm, the Central Overland California and Pike's Peak Express Company, agreed that the undertaking was a good idea. Hoping to gain a million-dollar government contract to carry mail over the central route, the company would invest $700,000, only to see its 18-month endeavor, begun on April 3, 1860, end in failure when the telegraph became a faster method of communicating.

In its heyday, the Express ran day and night, summer and winter, relaying mail by horse and rider. New riders, running east and west, took over every 75 to 100 miles (120 to 160 kilometers). Each got a fresh horse every 10 to 15 miles (16 to 24 km). At one time, the company owned 400 horses: thoroughbreds, mustangs,

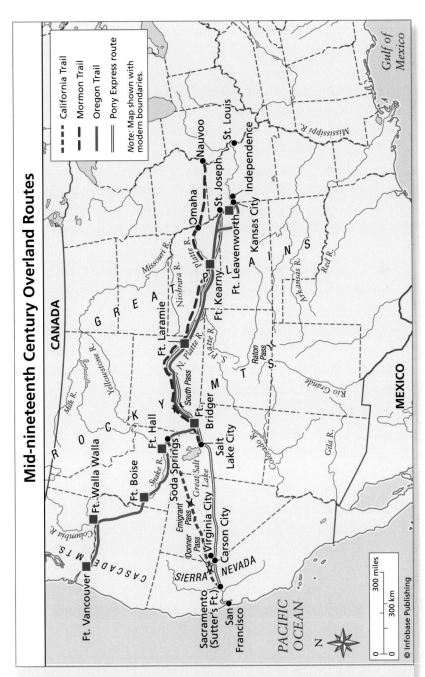

Mid-nineteenth Century Overland Routes

Legend:
- California Trail
- Mormon Trail
- Oregon Trail
- Pony Express route

Note: Map shown with modern boundaries.

Gulf of Mexico

Mississippi R.

St. Louis

Nauvoo

St. Joseph

Independence

Omaha

Kansas City

Ft. Leavenworth

Ft. Kearny

CANADA

GREAT PLAINS

Missouri R.

Niobrara R.

Platte R.

Ft. Laramie

N. Platte R.

S. Platte R.

South Pass

Ft. Bridger

Raton Pass

Arkansas R.

Red R.

Rio Grande

MEXICO

ROCKY MTS.

Milk R.

Yellowstone R.

Snake R.

Ft. Hall

Ft. Walla Walla

Ft. Boise

Soda Springs

Salt Lake City

Great Salt Lake

Emigrant Pass

Donner Pass

Virginia City

Carson City

Colorado R.

Gila R.

Columbia R.

CASCADE MTS.

Ft. Vancouver

SIERRA

NEVADA

Sacramento (Sutter's Ft.)

San Francisco

PACIFIC OCEAN

N

300 miles
300 km

© Infobase Publishing

As the U.S. border stretched towards the Pacific Ocean, settlers in the West longed to hear from relatives and friends who were back in the East. Because messages were often delayed when traveling by train or ship, the Pony Express used men on horseback to offer faster delivery. Buffalo Bill was their youngest rider.

pintos, and Morgans. Approximately 165 stations were set up along its nearly 2,000-mile (3,218-km) route, from St. Joseph, Missouri, to Sacramento, California. In the summer, a half-ounce letter, costing five dollars to deliver, could reach across the route's farthest destination in 10 days. In winter, it might take from two to six days longer.

Riders for the Pony Express were paid $100 a month—a good income in the early 1860s. For William Cody to earn that kind of money, almost all of which would have been sent home to his widowed mother, was a godsend to the whole family. At 14, young Cody was the man of the house, even if he spent little time there.

According to legend (and little else), a man named Bob Haslam is credited with the longest ride ever made in the services of the Pony Express. It is said that he rode 370 miles (595 km), from Friday's Station to Smith Creek and back, in one continuous run. Cody claimed that he, not Haslam, had the most notable run. In his 1879 autobiography, *The Life of Hon. William F. Cody, Known as Buffalo Bill, the Famous Hunter, Scout, and Guide, An Autobiography*, Cody wrote of his bone-jarring ride:

> One day when I galloped into Three Crossings, my home station, I found that the rider who was expected to take the trip out on my arrival, had got into a drunken row the night before and had been killed; and there was no one to fill his place. I did not hesitate for a moment to undertake an extra ride of eighty-five miles to Rocky Ridge, and I arrived at the latter place on time. I then turned back and rode to Red Buttes, my starting place, accomplishing on the round trip a distance of 322 miles [518 km].

Such a run by any man (let alone a boy) would have been astounding. Incredibly, Alexander Majors, Cody's employer, wrote in his 1890 memoir, *Seventy Years on the Frontier*, that the distance traveled without a stop (except for meals and to change horses) was actually 384 miles (617 km)! Conveniently, that would be 14 miles (22 km) longer than the run by Bob Haslam.

Did Cody gallop 384 miles, or even 322 miles, for the Pony Express? Indeed, did William Frederick Cody ride for the Pony Express at all? Were the youngster's adventures in the saddle, in which he did what every western kid longed to do—ride for a glamorous outfit that was destined to make history—merely a typical Westerner's tall tale? Maybe—or maybe not!

THE TRUTH BE TOLD

Most of what is known of William Cody's early life comes from his first autobiography, published in 1879, when the scout was 36 years old. Written during the height of Will Cody's theatrical career as Buffalo Bill, the book is filled with vignettes, thrilling adventures, daredevil doings, and the writer's conquest of the prairies. Its accuracy was questioned from the moment it appeared in print, and biographers to this day continue to poke holes in the autobiography's many anecdotes.

Indeed, from the first page, the first paragraph—actually, the first sentence—there is cause to question the accuracy of his memoirs. "My *debut* upon the world's stage occurred on February 26, 1845," the budding author wrote. Yet, for an author to get the date of his own birth wrong—either because of a lapse in memory, a lack of attention to detail, or simply a typographical error—is, at the least, disconcerting. William Frederick Cody, alias Buffalo Bill, was born in 1846, not 1845.

When it comes to *The Life of Hon. William F. Cody* and what was said about its author's Pony Express experiences, there is much to question. Cody states that the Pony Express began in 1859. Its first run was actually in April 1860. Cody declares in his autobiography, "Excitement was plentiful during my two years' service as a Pony Express rider." The Express ran for just 18 months. Helen Cody Wetmore, William Cody's sister, in a biography of her brother, *Buffalo Bill: Last of the Great Scouts*, stated that young Will rode three times a day for three months. No rider had that kind of schedule. Finally,

Wetmore asserted that William Cody wrote home with exciting accounts of his days in the saddle. In reality, at that time in his life, Will was illiterate; he couldn't even sign his name.

In *Fact Versus Fiction in the Kansas Boyhood of Buffalo Bill*, written by Dr. John S. Gray (a medical doctor turned historian), the author deconstructed Cody's childhood in an attempt to separate fact from fiction. In Gray's opinion, *The Life of Hon. William F. Cody* "features such chronological confusion, absurd heroics, and sheer impossibilities as to defy anyone's credulity." The doctor concludes, "There is but one tiny ember beneath these billows of smoke: for two months in the summer of 1857, the 11-year-old Cody rode as a messenger boy for Russell, Majors, and Waddell within a three-mile radius of Leavenworth. There seems no point in resisting the inevitable; Bill's pony riding represents another spate of fiction."

FACT AND FICTION

Yet, to dismiss William Cody's 1879 autobiography as mere hype, the spouting forth of tall tales that western men loved to relate, would be a mistake. There is much in Buffalo Bill's autobiography that should be taken, if not at face value, as essential truth.

Cody, it can be pointed out, never claimed to have ridden 384 miles for the Pony Express—Alexander Majors was the one who asserted that. Interestingly, Majors later protested exaggeration in the editing of his 1890 book, the likely juggling of figures to make it look like Cody established a record. In his autobiography, Cody related only one Pony Express ride, one in which the narration was obviously written by him. In numerous instances, it is evident that along the way from a difficult-to-decipher, handwritten manuscript to the final publication, much misreading probably took place.

Furthermore, in many cases, army records corroborate Cody's frequent hunting, scouting, and Plains Indian fighting claims presented in his autobiography. It is true that in the telling of his adventures Cody is quick to praise army personnel to place them in a most favorable light. Nevertheless, it is unfair to suggest, as at least one biographer has, that army officers signed off on exaggerated Cody claims for some kind of mutual agreement.

It is also worth noting that at numerous times, at the very moment when Cody would be expected to inflate a story, he is decidedly modest. Cody was once awarded an extra $100 for extraordinary services by the army as a trailer and fighter in the pursuit of American Indians. The army's entire train of command, up to and including the secretary of war, had to approve the grant, a recognition no other scout could boast. Yet in all the voluminous Buffalo Bill literature that exists, there is no mention of the award. William Cody did not brag of it.

Finally, if Cody sought (in his first autobiography) only to write in praise of his heroic and adventurous deeds, to convey the most positive of images, it is difficult to explain why, as an author, he didn't hesitate to expound on events decidedly unflattering. Upon the death of his mother in 1863, Cody wrote, "I entered upon a dissolute and reckless life—to my shame be it said—and associated with gamblers, drunkards, and bad characters generally. I continued my dissipation about two months and was becoming a very 'hard case.'"

Yet exaggeration and tall telling do exist in much of what William Cody wrote about himself, never mind what others wrote of him during his life. Perhaps this was to be expected, as William Cody transformed himself into Buffalo Bill and became, for a time, possibly the most famous man in the world. As Cody sought, in the last half of his life, to promote through theater and showmanship a heroic, romantic image of the Wild West that he himself did much to subdue, it is perhaps inevitable that fact and fiction should merge and become, at times, indistinguishable.

BLEEDING KANSAS

William Cody (called Will or Willie by his family) was born on February 26, 1846, in Scott County, Iowa. His early childhood reflected the adventures and misadventures of a rural boy growing up on the border of what then passed as civilization and the wild frontier lying just to the west. "Even at an early age my adventurous spirit led me into all sorts of mischief and danger, and when I look back upon my childhood's days I often wonder that I did not get drowned while swimming or sailing or my neck broken while I was stealing apples in the neighboring orchard," Cody wrote. "While living there [Scott County] I was sent to school, more for the purpose of being kept out of mischief than to learn anything."

In 1853, when Cody was seven years old, his family moved west to the new territory of Kansas. With the passage of the Kansas-Nebraska Act the following year, Will's new home soon became known as "bleeding Kansas." The territory's residents, torn between proslavery immigrants and antislavery rivals, immediately took out after one another, often with violent results.

When Will's father, Isaac Cody, a politically active antislavery advocate, rose at a political rally one evening to defend his position, he was not only shouted down, he was pulled down—and stabbed. Eight-year-old Will, who was with his dad at the time, related the September 18, 1854, incident: "He never finished this [his] sentence, or his speech. His expressions were anything but acceptable to the rough-looking crowd, whose ire had been gradually rising to fever heat, and at this point they hooted and hissed him, and shouted, 'You black abolitionist, shut up!' 'Get down from that box!' 'Kill him!' 'Shoot him!' and so on." Isaac was jabbed twice in the back with a Bowie knife.

In the next couple of years, Cody's father was essentially on the run, trying desperately to avoid direct contact with proslavery advocates who had sworn to kill him. "My father's indiscreet speech at Rively's brought upon our family all of the misfortunes and difficulties which from that time on befell us," Cody wrote. "As soon as he was able to attend to his business again, the Missourians began to harass him in every possible way, and keep it up with hardly a moment's cessation."

Indeed, during one evening it was learned that slavery proponents planned to lie in wait for Isaac as he returned home from visiting Grasshopper Falls, 35 miles (65 km) away. The word had to get to Isaac, lest he leave and be ambushed. Though nine-year-old Will lay

Even at a young age, William Cody's guts, talent, and endurance became apparent when he rode nine miles (14.4 kilometers) in the middle of the night to warn his father of an impending ambush. Later, when his father died, Cody went out into the world to find work and support his mother and six siblings.

in bed with a fever and chills, he got up and insisted on riding to warn his father. When assailants spotted Will as he galloped to sound the alarm, they charged after him. For nine miles, the men chased the frightened boy, as he, weakening, became sicker and sicker with every mile. Will finally reached a friendly farm. The would-be assassins turned and fled. As Will was taken from his horse, in a state of near collapse, he vomited all over the animal.

Isaac died on March 10, 1857, possibly from scarlet fever, though the stabbings that punctured a lung three years earlier were undoubtedly a contributing factor. The Cody family—a widowed mother and seven children—was left in desperate straits.

Given the extraordinary riding ability that young Will displayed on the night he rode to warn his father and his willingness to face danger, possibly death, while near death's door himself, it is not hard to imagine the boy taking up duties as a Pony Express rider a few years hence. Whether or not he actually did, it is clear from the nocturnal ride to save his father that William Cody was destined to lead a most adventurous life, a life as startling as it was real. Indeed, it is hard to understand why one who lived such a full and exhaustive life, much of it in the saddle as a man who was one with his horse, a centaur of the prairie, would ever want to fictionalize its amazing truths.

BOY PLAINSMAN

A year before his father's death in 1857, Will found himself in a rather uncommon place, for him anyway—school. How long he actually spent there is, like almost every event in Cody's early life, open to debate. The best evidence suggests no more than two and a half months at any one time, given the restless youth's wandering disposition.

In school, in spite of having demonstrated a fearless nature on numerous prior occasions, Will soon discovered he was not beyond experiencing the bullying of other boys, in particular one Steve Gobel, a classmate three years older. After weeks of Gobel's tormenting, the two lads came to blows during recess in the schoolyard. In the ensuing struggle, Will drew a pocketknife and stabbed Steve in the thigh. "I am killed! Oh, I am killed!" shouted the older boy, as Cody related in his 1879 autobiography. "The school children all rushed to the spot and were terrified at the scene. 'What's the matter?' asked one. 'Bill Cody has killed Steve Gobel,' replied another."

Although Steve was not seriously injured, Cody bolted, fleeing his club-wielding schoolmaster who had witnessed the struggle. In his escape, Will collided with John Willis, a wagon master in the employ of Russell, Major, and Waddell, proprietors of the largest freight train firm on the Great Plains. According to Cody, Willis, in an attempt to extradite him from a grim situation, made an offer that was hard to refuse: "Well, Billy, come along with me; I am bound for Fort Kearny; the trip will take me forty days. I want you for a cavallard driver."

That night, with Willis assuring Cody's mother, Mary, that her boy would be safely returned within six weeks, the trip was agreed to. The journey, out to Utah and back, in which he worked as a "boy-extra" (one who carried messages from wagon to wagon on mule-back), would profoundly shape Cody's life. According to Bobby Bridger, author of *Buffalo Bill and Sitting Bull*, "He [Cody] was entering the world of the bullwhacker; he was committing to a life of movement on the edge of the frontier; he was entering the world of massive logistics requiring fundamental knowledge of men, animals, and wagons." Indeed, Will was about to leave his boyhood behind.

As Cody would tell it, however, the trek out west was uneventful. "The trip proved a most enjoyable one to me, although no incidents worthy of note occurred on the way," he wrote in *The Life of the Hon. William F. Cody*. "On my return from Fort Kearny I was paid off the same as the rest of the employees."

Yet Bridger credits the trip with having an almost life-altering experience for Cody, one that turned a 10-year-old boy into a man. "He [Cody] had learned that in order to survive he would have to be cool-headed, clever, and creative," Bridger wrote. "Resourceful beyond his years, Will also knew instinctively that opportunities awaited him and he would need to develop extraordinary talents in order to create and meet those opportunities to succeed."

DEATH OF AN AMERICAN INDIAN

Within a brief time after Will's return home from his initial trip across the Plains, he was back out, again heading to Fort Kearny, this time working for cattle driver Frank McCarthy. If Will's first trip was uneventful, his second would be anything but.

Twenty miles from Fort Kearny, McCarthy and his party, having camped for dinner, were attacked by a large band of Pawnee Indians. After a fierce battle, with the bullwhackers outnumbered 10 to 1, the cattlemen fled under a shower of arrows. Desperate though they were, the fleeing men were able to build a small raft to carry a wounded comrade down the Platte River. Cody, being so young, was offered a spot on the float. He declined; he would manage for himself, thank you.

As stoic as Will was, he struggled to keep up with the older men as they waded, walked, and floated down the river at a fevered pace. Night fell. Will, though not lost, was clearly trailing his retreating comrades.

It is at this moment that Will's adventure becomes as interesting as it does questionable. Cody relates in *The Life of Hon. William F. Cody*:

> I being the youngest and smallest of the party, became somewhat tired, and without noticing it I had fallen behind the others for some little distance. It was about ten o'clock and we were keeping very quiet and hugging close to the bank, when I happened to look up to the moonlit sky and saw the plumed head of an Indian peeping over the bank. Instead of hurrying ahead and alarming the men in a quiet way, I instantly aimed my gun at the head and fired.... I was not only overcome with astonishment, but was badly scared, as I could hardly realize what I had done.

Will Cody, it seemed, had killed his first American Indian.

"From that time forward I became a hero and an Indian killer," Cody declares in his 1879 autobiography. "This was, of course, the first Indian I had ever shot, and as I was not more than eleven years of age, my exploit created quite a sensation."

Will would go on to kill a fair number of Plains Indians during his many years out west as a buffalo hunter and as a scout for the army. Being at the frontier of western expansion, it was, tragically, the sort of thing that happened as Americans pursued what they saw as their manifest destiny. Yet while Buffalo Bill would hunt American Indians, fight them in pitched battles, and, as a result, kill more than a few, he would never become an American Indian hater—far from it. The same could not be said of many others, soldiers and civilians alike, who engaged Plains Indian tribes in their desperate but futile struggle to maintain their hunting and nomadic ways.

WILD BILL HICKOK

Less than two weeks after his return to Kansas, Will was again looking to Russell, Majors, and Waddell for employment. This time the company was headed west to supply General Albert S. Johnston with desperately needed supplies, as the army commander prepared to engage Brigham Young's "Avenging Angels" in the infamous "Mormon rebellion." Will was still just 11 years old, and his reputation as the "boy Indian slayer" preceded him. Lew Simpson, one of the company's wagon masters, who was genuinely impressed with the boy, grabbed onto him.

It was on this trip that Will would meet and befriend a man with whom he was destined to share years of adventure, both on the trail and in the theater. Born James Butler Hickok, but soon enough known to the world as Wild Bill, the famous scout was a colorful character. In his first autobiography, Cody describes Hickok as "a tall, handsome, magnificently built and powerful young fellow, who could out-run, out-jump and out-fight any man in the train." George Armstrong Custer, who also knew Wild Bill, adds (as quoted in Bobby Bridger's account), "His hair and complexion were those of the perfect blonde. The former was worn in uncut ringlets falling carelessly over his powerfully formed shoulders."

Hickok could also shoot, of course, though as Cody explained in a deathbed interview, given in 1917, it was not because he was the quickest on the draw: "Bill was a pretty good shot but he could not shoot as quick as half a dozen men we all knew in those days. . . . But Bill was cool and the men he went up against were rattled I guess. Bill beat them to it. . . . It is easy enough to beat the other man if you start first."

The two, one a man and the other still a boy, cemented their friendship when Hickok, 10 years Will's senior, came to Will's rescue in another bullying incident. Evidently Simpson, a surly, overbearing type, took delight in tormenting Will. One evening over

While working as a boy-extra for a freight train company, Cody met a man who would become his big brother figure, friend, and protector. Wild Bill Hickok (*above*) was known as one of the best gunslingers of the West. He, like Cody, would become an American legend.

dinner, the wagon master demanded a favor. When the boy-extra did not start fast enough on the given task, Simpson slapped him in the face with the back of his hand, knocking Will off an ox yoke he was sitting on and sending him sprawling to the ground. Will, jumping to his feet, picked up a camp kettle full of boiling coffee and threw it at Simpson, scalding his face. As Will tells it in his 1879 autobiography, "He [Simpson] then sprang for me with the ferocity of a tiger, and would undoubtedly have torn me to pieces, had it not been for the timely interference of my new friend, Wild Bill, who knocked the man down."

When confronted by Simpson, Hickok responded (according to Cody), "It's my business to protect that boy, or anybody else, from being unmercifully abused, kicked and cuffed, and I'll whip any man who tries it on. And if you ever again lay a hand on that boy—little Billy there—I'll give you such a pounding that you won't get over it for a month of Sundays." Young Will, it seems, had acquired a protective big brother.

MULE BARRICADE

The next day, Simpson's bull train pressed on to Utah. Yet, not long after its departure, the caravan was intercepted by Brigham Young's Avenging Angels, who were determined to steal the supplies it carried. After driving off most of Simpson's cattle, the Mormons nonetheless allowed him to proceed on to Old Fort Bridger in the Rocky Mountains. There, with brutal winter storms coming, the party would need to hunker down.

At the fort, as supplies ran low, near-starvation conditions eventually took hold. Everyone was put on three-quarter rations, then half rations, and finally one-quarter rations. As Bridges details in *Buffalo Bill and Sitting Bull*, "Worn-out cattle, so poor they had to be propped up to be shot down, were killed for beef. When the cattle were gone they ate their mules."

In the spring of 1858, Simpson and his crew headed east again, to Fort Laramie. From there, the bullwhacker, now a brigade wagon master, took charge of two large trains with about 400 men and started off for Fort Leavenworth.

One morning, while moving back and forth between the two convoys (traveling approximately 15 miles, or 24 km, apart), Simpson, an assistant named George Woods, and Will were ambushed by a large Plains Indian war party. Knowing he and his two companions could not escape on their worn-out mules, Simpson jumped from his mount and ordered Woods and Cody to do the same. Without hesitation, according to Will's account in *The Life of Hon. William F. Cody*, "He [Simpson] then shot the three animals, and as they fell to the ground he cut their throats to stop their kicking. He then jerked them into the shape of a triangle, and ordered us inside of the barricade."

The bullwhackers, armed with Mississippi Jaeger rifles and a pair of Colt .45 revolvers, were able to drive off the first wave of American Indian raiders. The "hostiles" returned soon enough, however, pelting the mule barricade with piercing arrows. With the Plains Indians once more driven off, the trio, within their "animal fort," literally began to dig in, shoveling dirt over their dead mules. When night fell, the Plains Indian war party set fire to the prairie, hoping to burn Simpson's party out of its fortification. When the fire failed in its purpose, the trio of defenders once again staved off disaster.

The Plains Indians were prepared to wait out the three bullwhackers, starving them into submission. Yet they miscalculated. Having assumed that there was but one wagon train, the Plains Indians were surprised to find a second coming up behind them. After one last futile charge at the mule fort, the Plains Indians then disappeared out on the prairie. Simpson, Woods, and Cody had survived.

In February 1859, having returned to Kansas, Will acceded to his ailing mother's demand that he take a rest from his adventurous life and reenter school. Will, about to become a teenager, agreed to give it a try.

DUGOUT ORDEAL

Will stayed in school for what he claimed would be his longest run, two and a half months, before he was again out looking for adventure and money, this time in the form of gold. "The Pike's Peak gold excitement was then at its height, and everybody was rushing to the new gold diggings," Cody reported in his 1879 autobiography. "I caught

Wagons West

By the age of 13, Will Cody had seen more adventure traveling west from his home in Kansas than most men twice his age. In the employ of Russell, Majors, and Waddell, Cody made numerous treks, in one case as far as Denver. In his first autobiography, published in 1879, Cody takes pains to inform his readers as to just what a freight (wagon) train consisted of and the various jobs needed to make it move.

The wagons used in those days by Russell, Majors & Waddell were known as the "J. Murphy wagons," made at St. Louis specially for the plains business. They were very large and were strongly built, being capable of carrying seven thousand pounds of freight each. . . . These wagons were generally sent out from Leavenworth, each loaded with six thousand pounds of freight, and each drawn by several yokes of oxen in charge of one driver. A train consisted of twenty-five wagons, all in charge of one man, who was known as the wagon-master. The second man in command was the assistant wagon-master; then came the "extra hand," next the night herder; and lastly, the cavallard driver, whose duty it was to drive the lame and loose cattle. There were thirty-one men all told in a train. The men did their own cooking, being divided into messes of seven. One man cooked, another brought wood and water, another stood guard, and so on, each having some duty to perform while getting meals. All were heavily armed with Colt's pistols and Mississippi yagers, and everyone always had his weapon handy so as to be prepared for any emergency.

The wagon-master, in the language of the plains, was called the "bull-wagon boss"; the teamsters were known as "bull-whackers"; and the whole train was denominated a "bull-outfit." Everything at that time was called an "outfit."

the gold fever myself, and joined a party bound for the new town of Auraria, on Cherry Creek, afterwards called Denver." Not knowing anything about prospecting, Will lasted but two months before giving up the effort and heading home to Kansas.

Not to be discouraged, however, in November, Will, along with a 23-year-old friend, Dave Harrington, set out west on a trapping expedition. Their outfit consisted of one wagon, a yoke of oxen, various provisions, and traps.

The pair made it as far as Prairie Dog Creek at the mouth of the Republican River in Kansas when one of the oxen slipped on the ice, dislocated a hip, and had to be shot. Unable to proceed, Cody and Harrington decided to hole up for the winter, hunting beavers in the vicinity. They built a dugout in the side of a hill, covered it with grass and soil, put in a fireplace, and gathered an extensive supply of wood. The two probably would have pulled through the season had Will not fallen on the ice chasing an elk, breaking a leg above the ankle. Cody recounted in his 1879 autobiography: "Not withstanding the great pain I was suffering, Harrington could not help laughing when I urged him to shoot me, as he had the ox, and thus end my misery. . . . 'I am not much of a surgeon,' said he, 'but I can fix that leg of yours, even if I haven't got a diploma.'"

Harrington's leg-setting aside, it was quickly decided that the older boy should start out for the nearest settlement, 125 miles (201 km) away, borrow a yoke of oxen, and come back for the wagon, its pelts, and Will. Young Will would have to remain in the dugout for the duration, at least 20 days by Harrington's estimation. With plenty of wood for a fire, lots of meat and other provisions within reach, and a can on a string and stick to get snow for water, it looked like boredom would be Will's only challenge as he waited out his rescue. It was not.

On the twelfth day of his confinement, Will was awakened from a sound sleep by a touch on his shoulder. His eyes fluttering open, he found himself staring into the face of a war-painted American Indian. It was none other than Rain-in-the-Face, whom Cody had met once before at Fort Laramie.

Rain-in-the-Face and his band, though agreeing to spare Will's life, relieved the boy of his rifle, pistol, cooking utensils, sugar, coffee, and matches. "[They] were polite enough to give me some of the

Rain-in-the-Face and Cody crossed paths several times in their lives, the first at Fort Laramie. The two met again when Cody, injured and vulnerable, was waiting for his friend to return with provisions during a hunting trip. Rain-in-the-Face later became known for his role in the Battle of Little Bighorn, otherwise known as Custer's Last Stand.

food after they had cooked it," Cody reported in *The Life of the Hon. William F. Cody*. The Plains Indians left Will with part of a deer, flour, salt, and baking powder.

With snow piling up throughout the region, it wasn't until the twenty-ninth day that Harrington made it back to the dugout with borrowed oxen. "Well old boy, you're alive, are you?" Harrington was to have said upon seeing his emaciated friend. "Yes; and that's about all," replied Will.

Gathering up their traps and furs, the two made it back to Junction City, sold everything, and arrived back home in March 1860, just in time to greet the gathering American tensions over slavery that would tear the country apart.

BUFFALO BILL

With the outbreak of the Civil War in April 1861, 15-year-old Will Cody chose to take up with a rough, revengeful crowd of law-breakers known as the Kansas "Jayhawkers." Though Cody un-doubtedly felt he was aiding the North in its attempt to preserve the Union, his actions in the following months had the stamp of anarchy and hooliganism. In effect, Cody would become a Great Plains juvenile delinquent—when he wasn't riding for the Pony Express, that is.

As the War Between the States got under way, frontier mi-litia on both sides took to fighting on their own terms, often purely for territorial dominance and revenge. They would raid, rob, and pillage one another's villages and towns. In "free" Kan-sas, antislavery forces took to calling themselves Jayhawkers. In the slave state of Missouri, proslavery forces were known as Bushwhackers.

Joining up with the Jayhawkers was a no-brainer for Cody. Proslavery partisans in Missouri had for years threatened his mother, his sisters, and his little brother. They had killed his fa-ther, Isaac. Cody couldn't wait to enlist in the "fighting." "A man by the name of Chandler proposed that we organize an indepen-dent company for the purpose of invading Missouri and making war on its people our own responsibility," Cody relates in his first autobiography. "He at once went about it in a very quiet way, and

When the Civil War started, Cody joined a band of violent antislavery men called the Jayhawkers. This group of men would often travel from Kansas, a free state, to Missouri, a slave state, and steal horses or incite trouble. *Above,* Union soldiers encounter slavery supporters in Kansas.

succeeded in inducing twenty-five men to join him in the hazardous enterprise." One of those "men" was Will Cody.

Leaving their homes in groups of no more than two or three, the Jayhawkers rendezvoused at a point near Westport, Missouri, on a chosen day. The gang then broke up, heading to various homesteads to steal horses. "He [Chandler] directed us to secretly visit certain farms and collect all the horses possible, and bring them together the next night," Cody reveals in his first autobiography. "This we did, and upon reassembling it was found that nearly every man had two horses. We immediately struck out for the Kansas line. . . . Some of the parties boldly took their confiscated horses into Leavenworth, while others rode them to their homes."

Cody admits in his book that his behavior constituted horse stealing, an illegal action even in time of war, but that seems not to have disturbed young Will at all. "Chandler plausibly maintained that we were only getting back our own, or the equivalent, from the Missourians, and as the government was waging war against the South, it was perfectly square and honest, and we had a good right to do it," Cody continues. "So we didn't let our consciences trouble us very much."

Cody's mother, however, saw her boy's activities for what they were, neither right nor honorable. At her stern urging, Cody was forced to abandon his Jayhawking exploits.

SPY SERVICE

Though Cody was away from home through most of his youth—as a boy-extra, a trapper, a gold seeker, a cattle driver, and maybe even as a Pony Express rider—he remained close to his mother, particularly after his father's death in 1857. Mary Cody's death, on November 22, 1863, from consumption (tuberculosis) thus hit Will hard. "Even as a pre-adolescent boy cast out upon the Great Plains with bulltrains, bullwackers, Indian raids, Pony Express bandits, and gun-slinging murderers, Mary Cody remained a stabilizing force in Will's life," Bobby Bridger wrote. "After her death Will lost his direction and entered a deleterious period of grief."

Though Cody had promised his mother he would not volunteer to fight in the Civil War as long as she lived, with her death, and having turned 18 on February 10, 1864, he was now "available."

Cody's induction into the 7th Kansas Regiment, known as Jennison's Jayhawkers, was anything but voluntary, however. When members of the regiment came to Leavenworth seeking recruits among hometown boys, Cody was suckered in. "Among them [the veterans] I met quite a number of my old comrades and neighbors, who tried to induce me to enlist and go south with them," he relates in *The Life of Hon. William F. Cody*. "I had no idea of doing anything of the kind; but one day, after having been under the influence of bad whisky, I awoke to find myself a soldier in the Seventh Kansas."

Although Cody promised his mother that he would not fight in the Civil War, he could not resist his love for his country and adventure and enlisted in the Union army shortly after her death. He would serve as a scout and sometimes as a spy.

Army records show that Cody enlisted on February 19, 1864. He is described as having brown hair and eyes, being of fair complexion, and standing five feet ten. In later accounts of his Civil War exploits, Cody would state that he had worked as a scout. On at least one occasion, that description would morph into being a scout/spy.

As the story goes, cloaked in a gray Confederate uniform, Cody stopped at a Missouri farmhouse, whereupon he saw a man, also dressed in gray, sitting at a table eating bread and drinking milk. As Cody relates in his first autobiography,

> He [the man] looked up as I entered, and startled me by saying: "You little rascal, what are you doing in those 'secesh' clothes?"
>
> Judge of my surprise when I recognized in the stranger my old friend and partner, Wild Bill, disguised as a Confederate officer.
>
> "I ask you the same question, sir," said I without the least hesitation.
>
> "Hush! Sit down and have some bread and milk, and we'll talk it all over afterwards," he said.

Hickok, to be sure, had been spying for the North. Before the two departed, he gave Cody some papers concerning Confederate movements to be taken back to his commanding officer. Though the tale seems melodramatic, such spying did indeed occur during the Civil War. As historian Don Russell pointed out, however, "The most fantastic part of the story is Wild Bill and Cody sitting down together with bowls of bread and milk."

MULE STAMINA

Cody served one year, seven months, and ten days with the 7th Kansas Cavalry. He was mustered out as a private on September 29, 1865.

Earlier, in the spring, Will had met a young woman, the one he would eventually marry. Much has been written about the courtship of dashing Will Cody and Louisa Frederici, a beautiful French girl. Where and when the two actually met, and under what circumstances, is open to question. In the most romantic variation on what took place, Helen Cody Wetmore, Will's sister, offers the following account, published in her biography, *Buffalo Bill: Last of the Great Scouts*:

> More than once, while out for a morning canter, Will had remarked on a young woman of attractive face and figure, who sat her horse with the grace of Diana Vernon. Now, few things catch Will's eye more quickly than fine horsemanship. He desired to establish an acquaintance with the young lady, but as none of his friends knew her, he found it impossible.
>
> At length a chance came. Her bridle-rein broke one morning; there was a runaway, a rescue, and then acquaintance was easy.

Will and Louisa were married on March 6, 1866, with the understanding that Will would give up his daredevil ways and settle down in search of domestic tranquility. It didn't happen. Failing at managing a hotel, Cody was soon heading west, seeking work at the end of the Kansas Pacific Railroad. Louisa, wanting none of the frontier life, remained behind in St. Louis.

In the winter of 1866–1867, Cody scouted between Fort Fletcher and Fort Ellsworth. In the spring of 1867, he met Lieutenant Colonel George Armstrong Custer, the man who would, in 1876, meet his death at the famous Battle of the Little Bighorn. Custer needed someone to scout for him and his party of 10 men bound for Fort Larned, 65 miles (104 km) across the Plains.

Cody showed up for duty mounted on an army mule. Custer was not impressed. Nonetheless, when the colonel condescendingly suggested that Cody select a horse instead, Cody politely assured Custer that his mule would match the pace of the horses.

For the first 15 miles (24 km), Custer's thoroughbred and the other officers' horses led the pack. Cody's mouse-colored mule, it

Jayhawkers and Bushwhackers

The Kansas-Nebraska Act of 1854 established, among other things, the territorial boundaries of Kansas and Nebraska. In so doing, it opened the land of both regions to legal settlement. Residents could decide, by popular vote, whether their future states would be free or slave. Quick enough, people on both sides of the controversy flooded into Kansas, hoping to influence the vote in their favor. Violence broke out immediately between free-state Jayhawkers and proslavery Bushwhackers. From 1854 to 1861, when Kansas entered the Union as a free state, the territory was known as "bleeding Kansas."

In one incident, not atypical, Benjamin Rice, a free-soiler, was arrested and imprisoned in the Fort Scott Hotel. When James Montgomery, a leader of the free-state forces, came to rescue Rice, he tangled with former deputy marshal John Little, a proslavery advocate. In the evening struggle, Little was shot dead.

In a passionate letter to Montgomery, Little's fiancée, Gene Campbell, wrote on January 4, 1859:

Listen to me. Today I heard that you said in a speech a few days ago that you were not sorry you had killed John Little. That he was not killed too soon. Can you before God say so? Oh the anguish you have caused.... A few days more and we were to have been married, then go south to trouble you no more....

But remember this. I am a girl, but I can fire a pistol. And if ever the time comes, I will send some of you to the place where there is "weeping and gnashing of teeth." You, a minister of God? You mean a minister of the devil, and a very superior one too. I have no more to say to you and your imps. Please accept the sincere regards of your future repentance.

In little over a year hence, the nation as a whole would experience similar agonies on a grand scale as it plunged into civil war.

seemed, had trouble keeping up. Custer repeatedly told Cody he had made a mistake, that he should have gotten a horse. Yet, when the party hit the sand hills (across the Smoky Hill River), the mule showed what it was made of, its endurance shining through. Cody led the rest of the way, continually outdistancing Custer and his fatigued horses.

At journey's end, Custer was so impressed with Cody that he offered to hire him as a scout any time the young man needed work. Cody, as the years progressed, would take up scouting as an occupation, with considerable success and notoriety.

TOWN FOUNDER

Though Cody had demonstrated little success in business when, after the Civil War, he failed at operating a hotel, the defeat in no way dampened his entrepreneurial spirit. Now, at 21, Cody wanted and needed to earn money, real money, if for no other reason than to impress his impressionable bride.

In August 1867, Cody quit scouting to team up with a man named William Rose, who had a grading contract with the Kansas Pacific Railroad near Fort Hayes. Together, the two formed a partnership, the purpose of which was to found a town in Kansas on the west bank of Big Creek, where the railroad was scheduled to cross. They hired a surveyor, bought supplies, and opened a store. The partnership would give away town lots to anyone who would build on them, keeping the choice corner locations for future profit. Cody brought his wife and a new daughter, Arta, to the town, where they lived in the rear of the store. Rose and Cody named their new town Rome.

Within weeks of its founding, the town seemed to be a worthwhile enterprise. "Our modern Rome, like all mushroom towns along the line of a new railroad, sprang up as if by magic, and in less than one month we had two hundred frame and log houses, three or four stores, several saloons, and one good hotel," Cody relates in his first autobiography. "Rome was looming up, and Rose and I already considered ourselves millionaires, and thought we 'had the world by the tail.'"

The euphoria was short-lived, however.

One day, a Dr. William E. Webb showed up, introducing himself as an agent for the railroad. Webb, seeing a flourishing town in the making, proposed that he be admitted into the existing partnership. When Rose and Cody rejected Webb's suggestion, the agent was quick to remind the two budding but naive entrepreneurs just how things really worked when it came to town founding and a railroad. "You know as well as I do," Webb told Rose and Cody, as quoted in Cody's autobiography, "that the company expects to make money by selling lands and town lots; and as you are not disposed to give the company a show, or share with me, I shall probably have to start another town near you. Competition is the life of trade, you know."

Indeed, the day after his meeting with Rose and Cody, Webb announced the formation of a new town, Hays City, to be located a mile east of Rome. The railroad, he told everyone, would locate its roundhouse and machine shops there. Immediately, Rome residents began tearing down their homes, board by board, and carting their materials to the new town site. "A ruinous stampede from our place was the result," Cody declared in his 1879 autobiography. "People who had built in Rome came to the conclusion that they had built in the wrong place . . . in less than three days our once flourishing city had dwindled down to the little store which Rose and I had built."

Louisa, disgusted with the fall of Rome, retreated to St. Louis. Rose and Cody took up where they had left off—grading for the railroad.

NAMED THE WINNER

Though the Kansas Pacific Railroad could be seen as the cause of Cody's failure in real estate, ironically, it also opened up for him a new, well-paying career that would come to define him. Needing to feed its crew of 1,200 hungry workers, the railroad, as it pushed construction ever west, was desperate for competent buffalo hunters to supply meat. Cody, having already obtained an excellent buffalo-hunting horse named Brigham and a breech-loading needle gun christened Lucretia Borgia, was ready and eager to take out after buffalo. Moreover, at $500 a month (excellent pay by any standards), Cody could certainly make a decent living for his family.

Hunting buffalo on the Great Plains, however, was hard work and hazardous. According to Cody's sister, Helen, "He [the buffalo slayer] must first scour the country for his game, with a good prospect always of finding Indians instead of buffalo; then when the game was shot, he must oversee its cutting and dressing, and look after the wagons that transported it to the camp where the workmen messed."

Cody was up to the task. In 18 months, after bringing down at least 12 buffalo a day (as his contract specified), he would claim to have killed 4,280 bison. In truth, the math doesn't add up, nor does the time he could actually have spent in the employ of Goddard Brothers, the railroad's meat supply subcontractor. No matter, Cody killed plenty of buffalo, so many in fact that railroad workers immortalized his buffalo hunting with a song, quoted in *Buffalo Bill and Sitting Bull*:

Buffalo Bill, Buffalo Bill
He never missed and he never will
Always aims and shoots to kill
And the company pays his Buffalo Bill.

Thus, it seems, this is how William Cody garnered the nickname "Buffalo Bill." "It clung to him ever after," wrote Helen Cody Wetmore, "and he wore it with more pride than he would have done the title of prince or grand duke."

Of course, Cody wasn't the only buffalo hunter on the Plains. Indeed, there were even other hunters by the name of Bill. One such person, known as Billy Comstock, took issue with Will Cody calling himself Buffalo Bill, claiming that he, Comstock, deserved the name more than Cody. To settle the matter, a contest was arranged to see who could kill the most buffalo.

The hunting ground was fixed near Sheridan, Kansas, and quite a crowd, consisting of officers, soldiers, plainsmen, and railroad men, gathered to see the event. Louisa and baby Arta were there as well.

According to Cody, writing in his memoirs, "We [both men] were to hunt one day for eight hours, beginning at eight o'clock in the morning, and closing at four o'clock in the afternoon. The wager was five hundred dollars a side, and the man who should kill the greater number of buffaloes from on horseback was to be declared the winner."

In the end, Cody would triumph—69 to 46. Both "Bills" ended their competition amicably, however, having taken a number of "champagne breaks" during the long, hot day. Yet from this day forward, there would be little doubt as to who Buffalo Bill was—he was William Frederick Cody.

4

CHIEF OF SCOUTS

When he wasn't hunting buffalo, Cody was scouting for the United States Army, an occupation that would eventually gain him the recognition necessary to take his career to a whole new level— playing himself as a prairie scout in theater productions around the country.

Army scouts became a necessity on the Great Plains in the 1860s and 1870s, when soldiers went in pursuit of "hostile" American Indians. The land looked flat, but it really wasn't. "Seemingly straight paths veered subtly in a direction which could lead a party far afield," wrote Louis S. Warren in his book, *Buffalo Bill's America*. "Few experiences were more frightening than searching for enemy Indians and becoming lost on the Plains in a thunderstorm or blizzard."

Thus, there developed the need for scouts, hunters, and traders who knew the local terrain and could guide army contingents through forbidding territory. Cody was quick to offer his services, to become an army scout who would not only guide but, when necessary, fight alongside infantry and cavalry. Eventually, Cody would get so good at what he did that he would become "king of them all" and be appointed chief of scouts.

In one defining episode, in the summer of 1868, Cody demonstrated extraordinary courage and endurance. General Philip Sheridan, out in pursuit of Kiowa and Comanche Indians, needed a rider to take urgent orders to a distant fort. Since several couriers had

Cody's experiences as a Civil War scout and a Pony Express rider made him an asset to the U.S. Army when searching for American Indians. Cody, skilled and brave, took on assignments other scouts were afraid to accept and was quickly promoted for his efforts.

already been killed in their attempt to ride through unfriendly territory, Sheridan found it impossible to find a runner. Cody, learning of the general's predicament, stepped forward.

In carrying out his perilous task, Cody would travel almost 350 miles (563 km) in less than 60 hours. "Like many of the best scouts, he opted to travel at night to decrease the chances of being seen by Indians," Louis S. Warren reported. "Beginning at Larned, 'after eating a lunch and filling a canteen with brandy,' he tied one end of a leather thong to his belt, and the other to his mount's bridle. When his horse stepped in a prairie dog hole and Cody fell off several miles along the route, the thong kept the animal close at hand."

During the last leg of Cody's endurance run, he was given a mule to ride. As Cody bent at a stream for a drink, the mule ran away from him. The animal, in a frustrating tease, kept a little jog ahead of Cody, just out of reach. "Mile after mile I kept on after that mule, and every once in a while I indulged in strong language respecting the whole mule fraternity," Cody wrote in his memoirs. After 30 miles (48 km) of an infuriating chase, Cody, as he neared his destination of Fort Larned, raised his rifle to his shoulder. "I blazed away, hitting the animal in the hip," Cody confessed. "Throwing a second cartridge into the gun, I let him have another shot, and I continued to pour the lead into him until I ran him completely laid out." Scouting not only had its dangers; it also had its frustrations.

BUFFALO STAMPEDE

For undertaking his momentous trek, Cody was appointed chief of scouts by the 5th Cavalry commander, General Sheridan. "In rapid succession Will Cody had gone from hotel manger to real estate entrepreneur, railroad grader, buffalo hunter, military courier and scout," observed Bobby Bridger. "The swift transition of occupations leading to his becoming chief of scouts of the celebrated Fifth Cavalry now placed him in the white-hot center of the Indian Wars."

From 1868 to 1872, William Cody would be employed as an army scout. He would make a good living, guiding brigades across the Great Plains, usually in pursuit of warring American Indian bands. There would be occasions, however, when Cody would offer his escort services to tourists and army officers who were out to chase buffalo. By this time, Cody's fame as both a scout and buffalo hunter had solidified. Most who met the flamboyant, buckskin-clad frontiersman called him Buffalo Bill.

Admired as Cody was by most of the army high command, there were times when the 24-year-old scout was willing to defy their authority, often in petulant ways. Though General Sheridan knew Cody as the most competent of scouts and hunters, the 5th Cavalry's new commanding officer, Colonel Royal, demanded a demonstration of Cody's skills.

According to legend, after a couple of days of marching, Royal asked Cody to find some buffalo, kill them, and bring the animal carcasses back to camp. "All right, Colonel, send along a wagon or two to bring in the meat," Cody responded, as related in *The Life of Hon. William F. Cody*. Royal replied, "I am not in the habit of sending out my wagons until I know that there is something to be hauled in; kill your buffalo first and then I'll send out the wagons."

Cody did as he was told, killing a half dozen buffalo. Wagons were then brought up. The next day, the colonel again asked Cody to go out and shoot more buffalo. Cody once more did what he was asked, going out for the buffalo without wagons. Then, as he wrote in his 1879 autobiography, "I managed to get seven of them headed straight for the encampment, and instead of shooting them just then, I ran them at full speed right into the camp, and then killed them all, one after the other in rapid succession."

Royal had witnessed the entire stampede and was furious, demanding from Cody an explanation. Cody responded that he had decided to let the buffalo provide their own transportation, rather than requesting wagons. Colonel Royal gave Cody no more trouble on the matter.

DOWNHILL WAGONS

General Sheridan's strategy in subduing warring American Indians was to pursue them during the winter, when the Plains tribes would be hunkered down in camps and thus vulnerable. To that end, General Carr, under orders from Sheridan, proceeded to Fort Lyon in November 1868 to outfit for a winter pursuit of Plains Indians in Colorado. Cody was his chief scout.

Upon arrival, Carr was informed that General William Penrose, with 300 men and a supply train composed of only pack mules (no wagons), had left three weeks earlier, heading west. Carr was ordered to follow with supply wagons and to overtake Penrose as soon as possible. Penrose, it was feared, would not have supplies necessary to survive the harsh winter conditions then sweeping the Great Plains.

On the third day out, Carr and his men encountered a blizzard, in a place aptly named Freeze-Out Canyon. The regiment had no choice but to camp and wait out the storm.

It was at this time that Carr ordered Cody to take four men and press through the storm to find Penrose's trail. They found one of the general's old camps, but they could go no farther. Cody returned to the regiment, informing Carr of his findings.

Pressing on the next day, through snowdrifts so thick that teamsters had to shovel a path for the wagons, Carr soon realized that Penrose, unencumbered with such wagons, had taken a more rugged route. Carr took a different way, one recommended by his chief scout, Cody. Carr proceeded easily until discovering they were on a high tableland, overlooking a pleasant creek below. The challenge before them was to get the wagons down the steep slopes.

Cody didn't flinch. He was sure his time with bullwackers would hold him in good stead. When Cody was asked how he intended to get the wagons down, he replied, as reported in his 1879 autobiography, "Run down, slide down or fall down—any way to get down."

After rough-locking the wagon wheels with chains, Cody started one wagon down the hill. "The wheel-horses—or rather the wheel-mules—were good on the hold-back," Cody explained in his autobiography, "and we got along finely until we nearly reached the bottom, when the wagon crowded the mules so hard that they started on a run and galloped down into the valley and to the place where General Carr had located his camp. Three other wagons immediately followed in the same way, and in half an hour every wagon was in camp, without the least accident having occurred."

Taking the wagons down the hill had secured for Carr's regiment valuable time in gaining on Penrose. As they pressed on, Cody, out in front, found three deserters from Penrose's expedition. They informed him of near-starvation conditions that Penrose and his men were undergoing. Three days later, when

Indian Scouts

Cody spent many years as a civilian scout in the West, hired under contract by the military. As such, he did not hold an army rank, did not receive discharge papers, and was not eligible for a pension. Cody was, however, given the coveted title of chief of scouts.

Indian scouts were also on the western frontier, most notably in the three decades after the Civil War. Such scouts usually enlisted in the military, were often given a rank, were paid an army salary, and were eligible for a pension. In 1866, an act of Congress authorized the hiring of American Indians as scouts:

> The President is authorized to enlist and employ in the Territories and Indian country a force of Indians not to exceed one thousand to act as scouts, who shall receive the pay and allowances of cavalry soldiers, and be discharged whenever the necessity of further employment is abated, at the discretion of the department commander.

American Indian scouts enlisted for various lengths of time. Navajo scouts typically enlisted for three- to six-month periods before being discharged. The same men might serve multiple enlistments. If an Indian scout served in the cavalry, he was required to sign up for a five-year period. In 1895, Indian scouts, as a class of military soldiers, were merged into the regular army.

American Indians served as scouts for a number of reasons. Many were seeking revenge against tribes they had fought for decades. Some

Cody, accompanied by Major Brown, arrived with a relief train of 50 pack mules loaded with provisions, they discovered that more than 200 horses and mules of Penrose's command had perished of fatigue or starvation. Cody's scouting had obviously saved many lives.

Above, these scouts were members of the Shoshone Tribe.

needed the money. Either way, their intimate knowledge of the terrain and the antagonist's thinking, plus their ability to live off the land, made them a valuable asset to the army. As General George Crook declared, as reported by Delbert Trew, "When we use Indian scouts we find hostiles. When we don't use Indian scouts we don't find hostiles."

KING OF THE BORDER MEN

Cody's heroic deeds on the Great Plains were not going unnoticed. He was becoming well admired, well respected, and, most importantly, well known for both his character and his actions. "Men wanted to befriend Cody because he knew no fear of Indians, outlaws, or wild horses," Bobby Bridger wrote. "He could outdrink them all without getting drunk, play cards all night, and wake them all up in the morning fresh and ready to ride. Few could outshoot him and none could outride him. He was the Wild West personified."

In July 1869, Cody met a man who was destined to take the scout's Wild West persona and make it famous throughout the country. Born Edward Zane Carroll Judson, but better known by his alias, Ned Buntline, the Easterner was a publisher, actor, playwright, and dime novelist. The colorful Buntline had once been hanged after shooting a jealous husband in a duel. Fortunately for Buntline, the rope broke.

Buntline arrived out west, at Fort McPherson, to, of all things, deliver a lecture on temperance (abstaining from or limiting one's drinking of alcohol). Upon hearing that Cody was to move out on an expedition in pursuit of Plains Indians, Buntline sought to put off the lecture and instead accompany Cody. In his 1879 autobiography, Cody describes his meeting with the famous novelist: "Just then I noticed a gentleman, who was rather stoutly built, and who wore a blue military coat, on the left breast of which were pinned about twenty gold medals and badges of secret societies. He walked a little lame as he approached us, and I at once concluded that he was Ned Buntline."

Initially Cody was hesitant in crediting Buntline with the ability to keep up with the expedition and worried that his visitor's medals might make a good target for a sharpshooter. Nonetheless, Cody changed his mind as it appeared that the novelist was more interested in the adventure than in writing about it. On the group's return to Fort McPherson, after having failed to engage any American Indians, Buntline asked Cody many questions about his background and his life on the Great Plains. The writer in Buntline, it seems, was never far afield.

After reading about Wild Bill Hickok's exploits in the West, New York writer Ned Buntline (*above*) headed out to meet the legend himself. When he failed to secure and interview Hickok, Buntline instead met Buffalo Bill Cody, and the two quickly became friends during a scouting expedition.

Indeed, upon his return to New York, Buntline sat down to compose. On December 23, 1869, there appeared in the *New York Weekly* the first installment of a new serial, *Buffalo Bill, The King of the Border Men*. Cody's notoriety would spread from the West to the East.

Also instrumental in Cody's rise to celebrity status was his champion, General Philip Sheridan. The general believed that to reinforce his own credibility with the eastern establishment, as well as European royalty (which was always fascinated with Plains Indians and the American West), his friendship with Buffalo Bill could be used to advantage. Sheridan sought to acquaint Buffalo Bill with his eastern "dude" friends, city dwellers unfamiliar with life on the range. The general would seek to induce members of the eastern upper class—and maybe even a crown head or two of Europe—to go west, where they could meet the famous Buffalo Bill, who would then lead them on buffalo hunting and American Indian scouting expeditions. It was a plan that would eventually result in spectacular success.

GRAND DUKE ALEXIS

In the next couple of years, Cody would continue to hunt buffalo and scout for the U.S. Army. Occasionally, wealthy eastern tourists would arrive, seeking Buffalo Bill's services as a guide or, in some cases, just to meet the famous Westerner. In January 1872, however, there appeared at the North Platte a visitor who surpassed all before him in status and position. The man's trip, carefully arranged by General Sheridan, would provide the 24-year-old Grand Duke Alexis, third son of Alexander II, czar of all the Russias, the time of his life and, not incidentally, launch Buffalo Bill on a road to national stardom.

This was to be no ordinary buffalo hunt. As part of the "entertainment," the army asked Cody to find the Sioux chief Spotted Tail and convince him to come to the buffalo hunter's camp, along with 100 of his warriors, painted for the occasion. Cody knew Spotted Tail and agreed to the plan, but, as historian Don Russell pointed out, "The trip was not without danger, for however friendly Spotted Tail might be at any particular time, some of his young men might be capable of killing a lone white man for his gun and horse if given the opportunity." Cody did reach the Indian village safely, and Spotted Tail, when informed of the Army's request, readily agreed to join the show, to put on a buffalo hunt and war dance.

Evidently, Buffalo Bill and Grand Duke Alexis got along famously. Early one morning, the hunters, accompanied by a huge entourage, set out on their mission. Soon, a herd was spotted. The purpose, of course, was for the grand duke to shoot a buffalo. Bobby Bridger recounted:

> The royal was placed close to Cody as the group of men charged into the herd. When Cody helped the Grand Duke negotiate himself to within twenty feet of the herd, the young man emptied his six-shooter without hitting an animal. Cody promptly rode up beside the Grand Duke and exchanged pistols with him. Alexis fired six more shots without hitting a single buffalo. Moving quickly to prevent the herd from escaping, Cody rode close to Alexis again, offered "Lucretia," and yelled for the Russian to follow his lead. . . . Cody shouted to Alexis to shoot and the big bull fell in his tracks.

Upon achieving his objective, the grand duke was said to have raised the buffalo's tail in the air (it had been cut off as a souvenir by a member of his hunting party) and let go "a series of howls and gurgles like the death song of all the foghorns and calliopes ever born," according to Don Russell. Soon enough, the entire expedition retired to celebrate further with bottles of champagne in honor of Grand Duke Alexis, who had killed his first buffalo.

5

ON STAGE

With the celebrity hunt for buffalo on the North Platte over, Grand Duke Alexis headed back to Russia, via New Orleans. Cody turned east, to New York with a stop in Chicago.

General Sheridan, ever the Buffalo Bill supporter, reminded Cody that Gordon Bennett II, an extremely wealthy eastern newspaper heir, had invited Cody to New York for a visit, offering to host his stay. The publisher sent Cody $500 for expenses, and Sheridan arranged for a 30-day pass. A free railroad ticket was secured, and in February 1872, Cody arrived in Chicago.

Taken to the department store Marshall Field's by the general's brother, Colonel Michael Sheridan, Cody was fitted for a suit of clothes. Upon looking at himself in the mirror, he contemplated cutting his hair to match his new, more cosmopolitan look. Fortunately, he was convinced by Colonel Sheridan to refrain from clipping his long, flowing locks in order to maintain his frontier image.

Upon his arrival in New York City, Cody looked up his old acquaintance Ned Buntline. Ned, being a born opportunist, was quick to see advantage in Buffalo Bill's popularity and acclaim. In no time, Buntline arranged for the dime novel *Buffalo Bill, The King of Border Men* to be turned into a play, to commence at the Bowery Theater. The production would star J.B. Studley as Buffalo Bill. Within days of the opening, the show was playing to packed houses.

One evening, Ned took Cody to see the play. "What might have been in Buffalo Bill's mind as he saw himself portrayed on stage?" Bobby Bridger wrote. "It must at first have seemed like an incredible nightmare that such a distorted version of his life should be the subject of a play and that such a drama would appeal to New York audiences."

The audience, however, upon hearing that the real Buffalo Bill was in the theater, went wild and demanded that the frontiersman acknowledge their applause. Cody was escorted to the stage, where he stood frozen in place.

"I looked up, then down, then on each side, and everywhere I saw a sea of human faces, and thousands of eyes all staring at me," Cody recalls in *The Life of Hon. William F. Cody*. "I confess that I felt very much embarrassed—never more so in my life—and I knew not what to say. I made a desperate effort, and a few words escaped me, but what they were I could not for the life of me tell, nor could any one else in the house."

The theater manager, undeterred by Cody's stammering, nonetheless offered him $500 a week to take the part of Buffalo Bill himself. "I thought he was joking," Cody declared in his autobiography. "I told him that it would be useless for me to attempt anything of the kind, for I never could talk to a crowd of people like that, even if it was to save my neck, and that he might as well try to make an actor out of a government mule."

"THERE'S MONEY IN IT"

In the spring of 1872, Cody returned to Fort McPherson to resume his scouting duties. Almost immediately, the frontiersman once again found himself fighting and chasing Plains Indians. For his courage in such exploits, Cody, in an extraordinary act for a civilian, received the Medal of Honor from Congress on May 22, 1872.

In addition to scouting and hunting, Cody was selected as a Democratic candidate for the Nebraska legislature in the fall of 1872. He won, beating his heavily favored Republican opponent by just 44 votes. When the now "Honorable" William Cody failed to claim his seat, however, his opponent took office.

Throughout the summer and into the fall, Cody had continued to receive letters from Ned Buntline imploring him to head east and

Written in four hours by Ned Buntline and a few hired clerks, *Scouts of the Prairie* featured Cody and his friend Texas Jack on the Chicago stage. The melodrama involved Cody and Texas Jack shooting and battling American Indians.

play himself in the theater. "There's money in it and you will prove a big card, as your character is a novelty on the stage," Buntline kept telling the scout, as quoted by Bobby Bridger. Buntline was sure he could teach Cody to overcome his fear and face an audience of "five thousand as easily as a half a dozen." Giving in to temptation, Cody and a friend, Texas Jack, a scout who was far more eager than Cody to try the stage, arrived on December 12 in Chicago, where they were met by Buntline.

The melodrama the Westerners were to star in, *Scouts of the Prairie*, was scheduled to open on December 18 at Chicago's Nixon's Amphitheater. There were two significant problems, however. The play had yet to be written, and the cast had yet to be selected. Buntline, without panicking, sequestered himself and a bunch of hired clerks in a hotel room and, supposedly, produced the play in just four hours. Of course, getting the stage-frightened pair of scouts to commit the script to memory would be yet another hurdle to overcome. After an all-night session, Cody and Jack had memorized just a few lines.

Opening night drew a huge crowd and, according to Joseph G. Rosa and Robin May in *Buffalo Bill and His Wild West*, "The 'presence of 2,200 bad breaths and twice as many unclean feet' encouraged the scouts to do their best." Early in the performance, Cody froze up, completely forgetting his lines. Buntline, who had a role in the performance, quickly turned to Cody and asked, "Where have you been, Bill? What has kept you so long?" Cody took the cue and proceeded to ad-lib the rest of his performance, telling the audience of his many western adventures. The multitude went wild.

In the process, Cody had struck gold, a formula for stage presentation that would allow him to tell the truth, albeit embellished with "tall tales." Through anecdote, Cody would play a real frontiersman playing the part of an actor playing the part of a frontiersman.

THE BUFFALO BILL COMBINATION

Not surprisingly, critical reviews of *Scouts of the Prairie* were less than flattering. Indeed, some descended into outright ridicule.

"The only originality in the piece itself is the grotesque combination of absurd elements," sniffed one reviewer, as quoted in *Buffalo Bill's Wild West* by Joy S. Kasson. "There is scarcely a vestige of a plot. The characters are mainly Indians and trappers, who repeatedly amuse themselves by fierce and fatal combats." Dialogue from the play amply supports the reviewers' criticism: "We'll wipe the Red Skins out"; "Then burn, ye cussed Dogs, burn"; "The cage is in here but the bird has flown"; "I'll not leave a redskin to skim the Prairie."

Yet, Cody was, as time went on, clearly on to something, something new in theater performance. He was opening himself up to his audience, breaking down that "fourth wall" that supposedly prevents an actor from ever communicating with those in the seats. If he was not an actor, he was rapidly becoming a showman, a term that would come to define him. As the troupe moved to Boston, New York, and Philadelphia, patrons jammed theaters. They didn't care about what *Scouts of the Prairie* may have lacked in plot; they came to see Buffalo Bill, the real deal, a famous western scout willing and able to open up to them, to tell it like it is.

After the theater season ended in early 1873, Cody headed west to resume his duties as a scout, but $6,000 richer. Cody was not particularly happy with the amount he had received, feeling that Buntline was holding back money owed him. When the 1873–1874 season opened, Cody got rid of Buntline and brought in a new manager, John Burke. The two would call their new theater production the Buffalo Bill Combination.

In the theater world, a combination is a traveling theatrical troupe. It performs one play and travels from place to place, renting theaters and putting on performances. In contrast, a stock company stays in a fixed location, offering a repertory of frequently changing plays. With the combination, Buffalo Bill's fame only grew greater. In a typical season, from October to the following May, he toured the East Coast. During late spring and summer, Cody headed back west to scout and hunt buffalo.

All seemed to be going well for William Cody, as a scout and an actor, until the evening of April 20, 1876. Cody was performing in Springfield, Massachusetts, in a new play, confusingly titled

Scouts of the Plains. Just before the performance began, Cody was handed a telegram informing him that his only son, five-year-old Kitty (named after Kit Carson, another legendary scout), was seriously ill in Rochester. Cody played the first act, then rushed to grab a nine o'clock train. The next morning, Kitty died in his father's arms of scarlet fever.

DUEL WITH YELLOW HAND

Cody ended his 1876 theatrical season early and again headed west. The U.S. Army's war on the Plains Indians was reaching an apex, and Cody wanted to be in on any fighting that took place.

In early June, Colonel George Armstrong Custer, as head of the 7th Cavalry, moved out from Fort Abraham Lincoln (in what is now North Dakota) bound for the Yellow River country in Wyoming. Two other regiments, one from the north and the other from the south, were also converging on the region. As Custer approached the area, his scouts informed him that hundreds of American Indians were somewhere nearby. Custer would soon discover that while the scouts were right about an American Indian presence, they were wrong, dead wrong, about their numbers. Camped in a grassy valley, later to be known worldwide as the Little Bighorn, were not hundreds but upward of 5,000 Cheyenne and Sioux.

Custer's attack on peacefully gathered tribes of Plains Indians on June 25 would go down as the worst defeat suffered by the U.S. Army in a single battle since the Civil War. Custer was killed, as were the more than 200 men in the five companies with him. When word spread to the East Coast and beyond about what had taken place at the Little Bighorn, the country rose up in indignation. "Custer Avengers" flocked to Sioux lands, eager to engage in any military action. One, however, was already there—William F. Cody.

On July 1, Cody, while out scouting with the 5th Cavalry near a place called Warbonnet Creek, discovered a large Cheyenne war party. He hurriedly rode back to his outfit, whereupon he suggested to the cavalry commander, Wesley Merritt, that he be allowed to take other scouts and cut off the main body of Cheyenne coming over a

Dime Novels

The dime novel, which in most cases sold for 10 cents, originated with the publishing of *Maleaska, the Indian Wife of the White Hunter*, by Ann S. Stephens, on June 9, 1860. The book was published by Beadle & Adams as part of the Beadle's Dime Novels series. Essentially, dime novels, roughly 6 ½ by 4 ¼ inches, contained a hundred pages of lurid, outlandish, melodramatic stories with double titling, such as *Prairie Prince, the Boy Outlaw; or, Trailed to His Doom*. It is said that dime novelist Ned Buntline wrote six such novels a week when at his peak, earning $20,000 a year. Many dime novels featured Buffalo Bill as their main character.

According to Don Russell, the following are a few titles spotlighting Buffalo Bill as protagonist:

Buffalo Bill's Buckskin Braves; or, The Card Queen's Last Game
Buffalo Bill's Grip; or, Oath-bound to Custer
Buffalo Bill's Bonanza; or, The Knights of the Silver
Buffalo Bill's Swoop; or, The King of the Mines
Buffalo Bill's Secret Service Trail; or, The Mysterious Foe
Buffalo Bill's Big Four; or, Custer's Shadow
Buffalo Bill's Double; or, The Desperado Detectives
The Hercules Highwayman; or, The Mounted Miners of the Overland
Buffalo Bill's Brand; or, The Brimstone Brotherhood
Buffalo Bill's Boys in Blue; or, The Brimstone Band's Blot-out
Butterfly Billy, the Pony Rider Detective; or, Buffalo Bill's Boy Pard
Buffalo Bill's Buckskin Braves; or, The Card Queen's Last Game
The Three Bills—Buffalo Bill, Wild Bill and Band-box Bill; or, The Bravo in Broadcloth
Buffalo Bill on the War Path; or, Silk Lasso Sam, the Wil-o'-the-Wisp of the Trails
Buffalo Bill's Scout Shadowers; or Emerald Ed of Devil's Acre
Buffalo Bill's Body-guard; or, The Still Hunt of the Hills
Buffalo Bill and His Merry Men; or, The Robin Hood Rivals

Dime. BEADLE'S New York Library

ENTERED AT THE POST OFFICE AT NEW YORK, N. Y., AT SECOND CLASS MAIL RATES.

Vol. XXIV.   Published Every Wednesday.   Beadle & Adams, Publishers,   98 WILLIAM STREET, N. Y., August 20, 1884.   Ten Cents a Copy. $5.00 a Year   No. 304

TEXAS JACK,

THE PRAIRIE RATTLER; or, THE QUEEN OF THE WILD RIDERS.

A Romance in the Life of a Real Hero—John B. Omohundro—Texas Jack—and a Tale of the Southwest Border.

BY HON. WM. F. CODY—"Buffalo Bill,"

AUTHOR OF "THE GOLD BULLET SPORT," "KANSAS KING," "DEADLY EYE," "THE PHANTOM SPY" ETC., ETC.

"YES, IT IS MY LOVELY RENA THAT IS COMING BACK TO ME AND BY HER SIDE RIDES THAT PRINCE OF TEXANS, WHOM MEN CALL THE THUNDERBOLT."

Dime novels, a popular and cheap form of entertainment, turned Cody into a legend.

ridge. Given permission, Cody and his men soon found themselves engaged in a lively skirmish with a number of Cheyenne. According to Cody, as stated in his 1879 autobiography, "One of the Indians, who was handsomely decorated with all the ornaments usually worn by a war chief when engaged in a fight, sang out to me in his own tongue: 'I know you, Pa-he-haska; if you want to fight, come ahead and fight me.'"

Exactly what took place in the next few moments, as Cody battled (dueled, he would later claim) with Yellow Hand, is open to dispute. According to Bobby Bridger, "Cody had so successfully mastered the art of dramatically blurring reality his autobiographical account of the actual 'duel' is a classic example of the effects of the theater on actual historical events in his life. Controversial even to this day, the fight between Cody and the Cheyenne warrior remains one of the great myths of the 19th century American West."

Cody, in a fierce but short struggle, killed Yellow Hand. He claims that he then "scientifically" scalped the warrior in about five seconds. Finally, as he states in his autobiography, "[I] swung the Indian chieftain's top-knot and bonnet in the air and shouted: 'The first scalp for Custer.'"

KISSING THE GIRLS GOODBYE

Not surprisingly, when Cody returned to the stage in the fall of 1876, he took his recent American Indian warring experiences with him, particularly his encounter with Yellow Hand. In no time, a drama called *The Red Right Hand; or Buffalo Bill's First Scalp for Custer* was staged in a theater. The production was a five-act play, described as having no head or tail, one in which it made no difference at which act the performance commenced. It was "gunpowder entertainment" at its best.

As the play moved from town to town, Cody took to advertising its presence by placing the scalp and headdress of Yellow Hand in store windows. Under pressure from local clergy and the press, however, the practice was soon stopped. It seemed too gruesome for eastern sensitivities.

Not so, perhaps, on the Pacific Coast, in the real West. Cody decided to head to California with his Buffalo Bill Combination.

Cody had been advised against making the trip. Why, the reasoning went, would anyone out west want to see enacted on the stage what was all around them? Yet, be it in San Francisco, California, or Virginia City, Nevada, Cody was a huge success. "Cody was first to discover what all producers of 'Westerns' ever since have proved," wrote Don Russell, "that the wholly imaginary and fictitious West of stage, book, or screen is most popular in the real West it mistakenly represents."

At the end of the 1876–1877 season, the Buffalo Bill Combination disbanded in Omaha, Nebraska. It was at that moment, however, that a seemingly innocent episode occurred that would haunt Cody's marriage for the rest of his life. Cody kissed his cast of ladies goodbye. Cody stated, as quoted in *The Lives and Legends of Buffalo Bill*:

> In paying off the company, I went to one of the rooms where the four ladies who were the four actresses of the company were waiting to receive their final settlement, which I paid them and got their receipts in full. The ladies were having a glass of beer in this room, and one or two of the gentlemen, members of the company, were in this room and we all had a glass of beer or two, or a drink of some kind, and we were talking of the past season, and we were jolly, laughing and talking. When I went to leave the party the ladies all jumped up and they said, "Papa, we want to kiss you good bye...." And I kissed them good bye and we were all laughing and joking.

One lady down the hall, Cody's wife, Louisa, heard of the incident and didn't laugh at all. Twenty-eight years later, the "kissing affair" would resurface in a bitter divorce trial.

SHOWMAN
EXTRAORDINAIRE

Being a hero of the Indian Wars only bolstered Buffalo Bill's stage successes, as he now moved back and forth between scouting and ranching out west in the spring and summer and traveling and performing in the fall and winter, usually in the East. Cody was making good money, but as the decade concluded, he began to tire of the effort to not only act but to put together a whole theater production, much of it on his own.

Furthermore, Cody was becoming acutely aware of the genre's limitations. On an indoor stage, shooting live ammunition was, of course, prohibited. In addition, while a couple of horses could be presented for effect, the animals had no room to run around even though riders were supposed to chase each other. After 10 years in the theater world, Cody not only required a change of scenery for himself, but he needed to elevate his entertainment production to a new level. In June 1882, he was given the chance.

As the story goes, Cody, the showman, was invited (or challenged) by leaders in his hometown of North Platte to put on a memorable Fourth of July celebration. The scout agreed, promising to make it an "Old Glory Blow Out," the likes of which no one had ever seen before.

Cody quickly realized that the theater had too many limitations to provide authentic, "Wild West" entertainment and developed his own outdoor production. Featuring demonstrations and competitions for various cowboy tasks, Cody's extravaganza was the precursor to modern rodeos.

Cody obtained permission to use the local, fenced-in racetrack for an outdoor arena. He planned to demonstrate how to kill buffalo, using a small local herd. Cody sent out 5,000 fliers announcing the event and offering prizes for riding, shooting, and bronco busting. The frontiersman hoped he would get maybe a hundred cowboy entrants; a thousand herdsmen showed up.

At the time, the term *cowboy* (though not the cowboy himself) was barely known, even in the West. Its origin is mysterious; one author suggested it came from the American Revolution, when cowboys were considered Loyalist guerrillas who stole Patriot cows.

No matter, in the West of the 1880s, cowboys were hired during the summer to facilitate the "roundup" of cattle, many of which had become widely scattered during the winter. As Cody explained in his 1879 autobiography, "In this cattle driving business is exhibited some most magnificent horsemanship, for the 'cow-boy,' as they are called, are invariably skillful and fearless horsemen—in fact only a most expert rider could be a cow-boy, as it requires the greatest dexterity and daring in the saddle to cut a wild steer out of the herd."

The Old Glory Blow Out, featuring riding, shooting, roping, bronco busting, and other feats, was a huge success. (Such an event would morph in the decades to come into the American rodeo.) While he would play out his theater obligations for the winter season, Buffalo Bill would also prepare to launch his Wild West extravaganza. The great outdoor-show era was about to begin.

TRIUMPH AND TRAGEDY

Cody wasn't the only one to recognize the success of the Old Glory Blow Out and what it could portend. A local sharpshooter and dentist named W.F. Carver, eager to get into the show business game himself, offered Cody $27,000 for a partnership in his new Wild West enterprise. Once accepted, the two booked the Omaha Fair Grounds in Nebraska for May 17, 1883. Their production, called The Wild West, Rocky Mountain and Prairie Exhibition, would include all manner of cowboy "showing off," as well as a reenactment of the dramatic horse exchanges of the Pony Express.

The show would also include American Indians—plenty of them. That such American Indians, many of whom had recently been in violent confrontation with whites all over the Great Plains, would agree to participate in the depiction of their warring ways may have seemed strange to some. Yet as far back as the 1860s, many tribes had concluded that Americans were fascinated by their culture and its depiction. According to Louis S. Warren, "In 1874, a group of Lakota performers charged settlers for admission to their dances at the opening of a Nebraska county. Selling their performances and images became standard. By 1877, Lakota, fresh from their campaigns against the Army, were charging white photographers $6 each for photographs." Cody would, in the next two decades, employ well over a thousand American Indians in his Wild West productions.

From Omaha, Cody and Carver took the Wild West to New York, then to Boston. The shows (afternoon events because there was no outdoor lighting) played in vacant lots and local fairgrounds. Audiences flocked to see "Cowboy Fun," as they eagerly absorbed lassoing, bareback pony races (one between an American Indian on foot with another on horseback), bucking and kicking ponies, and wild steer riding. Cody even took to mounting a wild bison named Monarch. No one in the show had been willing to ride the ornery bull, so Cody, ever up for a challenge, leaped aboard Monarch, rode a short distance, and was then bucked and thrown off. He was carried to the hospital, where the bruised and battered scout remained for two weeks.

The show's second year got off to a good start, with a crowd of 41,448 showing up on a single day in Chicago. Riding high on such success, Cody and his new partner, Nate Salsbury, decided to take the show on the road during the winter. They would head down the Mississippi River to New Orleans to attach themselves to the World's Industrial and Cotton Exposition of 1884. At Cincinnati, they hired a steamboat to convey the show southward.

It was on the ride south, in search of good weather, that the Wild West troupe encountered what would be its most devastating tragedy. Near Rodney Landing, Mississippi, their showboat collided with another river steamer. Within an hour, practically everything—equipment, weaponry, and animals—were at the bottom of the Mississippi River. Yet amazingly, Cody and the crew were able to recoup and open the show on time in New Orleans. Not being granted any reprieve, however, it then rained for 44 days straight. By winter's end, the Wild West was in debt to the tune of $60,000.

"LITTLE MISSIE"

New Orleans was not a total loss for Buffalo Bill's Wild West, despite the rain, poor attendance, and accumulated debt. Also appearing in the Crescent City was the Sells Brothers Circus. Some of its performers wandered over to the Wild West lot for a visit. One was a pretty, 25-year-old, diminutive young lady born Phoebe Ann Moses in Darke County, Ohio. Thanks to Buffalo Bill, she would soon become known to the world as Annie Oakley.

Annie was the fifth of seven children. At the age of nine, she took to helping feed the family by hunting game with an old black-powder 16-bore rifle. Her specialty was squirrels. To make every shot count, the girl soon learned to aim for the head in order to leave the animal's body intact. "It's a disgrace to shoot a squirrel anywhere but in the head because it spoils the meat to hit him elsewhere," she reportedly heard her brother say, as quoted in the *Lives and Legends of Buffalo Bill*. "I took the remark literally and decided, in a flash, that I must hit that squirrel in the head, or be disgraced."

As the years passed, Annie became better and better at picking off squirrels, always taking dead aim and shooting them in the eye. At times, she would take the surplus to a Cincinnati hotel owner named Jack Frost. Curious about this 15-year-old girl who was bringing in such perfectly slain squirrels, Jack proposed to arrange a shooting contest between Annie and a well-respected, professional marksman in the area named Frank Butler. Annie agreed, and the match was set for Thanksgiving Day 1875.

When Butler saw that his opponent was a girl under five feet tall, dragging a rifle bigger than she was, he almost bowed out, believing the whole setup was a joke. The contest, however, proceeded,

Annie Oakley was a special find for Cody and proved to be an immensely popular draw for his show. Trained at an early age to hunt and provide game for her family, Oakley became an expert markswoman, famed for her accuracy with a gun.

with each participant taking aim at 25 live pigeons. Annie won the match by one shot. Butler also won something, however—Annie's heart. A year later, the two were married. Butler, soon recognizing that his wife was the better shot, deferred to her in the shooting ring and instead spent his time promoting and managing her career.

Upon meeting Annie in New Orleans, Cody agreed to engage her for his Wild West on a three-day trial basis. According to *Women in History*, "At 90 feet Annie could shoot a dime tossed in mid-air. In one day with a .22 rifle, she shot 4,472 of 5,000 glass balls tossed in midair. With the thin edge of a playing card facing her at 90 feet, Annie could hit the card and puncture it with five or six more shots as it settled to the ground. . . . Shooting the ashes off a cigarette held in Frank's mouth was part of the Butler and Oakley act." "Little Missie," as Cody would come to call Annie, was hired for the Wild West's 1885 season.

OLD SITTING BULL

Annie Oakley was not the only prize recruit to come Buffalo Bill's way as the 1885 Wild West season began. From its inception, Cody sought to include in his extravaganza what Louis S. Warren called the most original frontiersmen of them all—American Indians. They, Cody felt, would always be his primary attraction, even more so than cowboys. Cody wanted, above all, for his Wild West to be authentic. Throughout the life of his extravaganza, he refused to call what he was doing a show. Yes, it was entertainment, but with a strong educational component. Referring to the Wild West as an exhibition emphasized its respectability, especially to middle-class audiences.

With American Indians a sure draw, in 1883 Cody wrote to the secretary of the interior about recruiting the best-known American Indian of them all. "I am going to try to get old Sitting Bull," he said to his partner, as quoted by Louis S. Warren. The Sioux chief was at the time confined to the Standing Rock Reservation, where he had surrendered in 1881. "If we can manage to get him our ever lasting fortune is made," Cody said.

Cody's request for Sitting Bull was denied; he was judged too dangerous to be let off the reservation. After all, to most Americans the Sioux chief was the "slayer of Custer," a blatantly false accusation

Annie Oakley

As good as Annie Oakley was, she was not without competition from other sharpshooters, including female competitors. One in particular, Lillian Smith, was put on the bill when the Wild West first toured England in 1887. She was only 15 years of age, and though loud and unrefined, she gave the 26-year-old Annie a run for her shots. Nonetheless, when Queen Victoria called both women to her box to honor their performances, Annie was the clear favorite. Today, few remember Lillian while nearly everyone has heard of Annie Oakley.

Of Oakley, Wild West press agent Dexter Fellows said, as quoted by Louis S. Warren, "Her entrance in the arena was always a very pretty one. She never walked. She tripped in, bowing, waving, and wafting kisses. . . . Her first few shots brought forth a few screams of fright from the women, but they were soon lost in round after round of applause. . . . It was she who set the audience at ease and prepared it for the continuous crack of firearms which followed."

In 1901, while traveling from Danville, Virginia, Annie's train suffered a head-on collision with a freight train. Oakley suffered a spinal injury that required five operations. For a time, she was left partially paralyzed. Annie did recover, but it would be years before she went back into show business, and never again for the Wild West. Though white-haired after the wreck, with a noticeable loss in her old spunky personality, "Little Sure Shot" nonetheless retained her marksmanship. Oakley continued to set records. In a contest in Pinehurst, North Carolina, in 1922, 62-year-old Annie hit 100 clay targets from the 16-yard mark.

On November 3, 1926, Annie Oakley died of pernicious anemia at the age of 66. Twenty years later, her remarkable life was celebrated in the Herbert and Dorothy Fields musical *Annie Get Your Gun*.

Cody understood that featuring American Indians in his touring extravaganza would entice large crowds to the shows. One of his most famous recruits was the Hunkpapa leader Sitting Bull, who joined the tour largely because it allowed him to spend time with Annie Oakley.

but one that would, nonetheless, make him in many folks' eyes a celebrity. They would want to see him all the more.

Yet in September 1884, authorities finally relented, and Sitting Bull was allowed to join other Sioux for a 15-city tour, though not one sponsored by Cody. At a St. Paul theater, the chief saw Annie Oakley in performance. He became mesmerized. According to Don Russell, Sitting Bull shouted "*Watanya Cecilia*," which meant "Little Sure Shot." After the show, the two exchanged photographs. The Hunkpapa Sioux supposedly adopted Oakley as his daughter.

When, at the end of 1884, John Burke was instructed by Cody to sign Sitting Bull, the publicist went searching for the famous chief. Upon entering his tepee, Burke spied a photograph of Annie Oakley. Grabbing the opportunity, Burke promised Sitting Bull that should he join the Wild West for its 1885–1886 tour, he would see Little Sure Shot every day. The chief took the bait. Sitting Bull would be paid $50 a month and a bonus of $125, and, most importantly, he was given the sole right to sell his photographs and autographs.

For Sitting Bull, the tour was an eye-opener, something that government officials may have anticipated when they thought about letting him go. "The white people are so many that if every Indian in the West killed one every step they took, the dead would not be missed," he said, as quoted in DeCost Smith's *Indian Experiences*. "I go back and tell my people what I have seen. They will never go on the war-path again."

AMERICA'S NATIONAL ENTERTAINMENT

By the end of the 1885 summer season, the Wild West exhibition had taken in more than $1 million, with $100,000 pure profit. For agreeing to tour with the exhibition, Buffalo Bill gave Sitting Bull a size 8 Stetson hat and a white trick horse. The Sioux leader declined to join in an 1886–1887 tour, however, feeling he was needed back on the reservation, where more American Indian lands were being taken away.

It was now clear that putting on the Wild West, and moving it from town to town, was becoming a logistical nightmare—or, depending on one's vantage point, an organizational triumph. Hauling around dozens upon dozens of animals, a cast and crew in the hundreds, and tons of equipment and baggage was not easy. Indeed, the Wild West required its own railroad train for transport. Each car, painted white, had the words "Buffalo Bill's Wild West" stenciled in gold on its side. According to Bobby Bridger, "When the 1886 season opened in St. Louis, the company mushroomed to 240 people organized military-style into crews working under the strict discipline of a single boss. The Wild West now had a sophisticated lighting system, seats, a canvas canopy and a canvas mural depicting the majestic mountain ranges of Wyoming."

All manner of frontier life had become a part of the Wild West. Among the many attractions there was a buffalo hunt, an American Indian attack on the Deadwood Stage, the Pony Express ride, and a presentation of Custer's Last Stand, in which some Lakota who had actually fought in the battle played a part. Of course, there was also Annie Oakley. In just one year, her stardom had begun to rival Buffalo Bill's. To promote her even further, Salsbury and Cody ordered $7,000 worth of posters and billboards for the 1886 season.

By the time the Wild West hit New York, settling on Staten Island for the summer season, it had become America's national entertainment. More than a million people would see the extravaganza—a few without having to pay. Cody, in a magnanimous giveaway gesture he may have picked up from Sitting Bull, took out ads in New York newspapers offering free tickets to any bootblack or newsboy who came to the ferry going to Staten Island. According to *Buffalo Bill and Sitting Bull*, "Fifteen hundred boys arrived on the arranged date and were greeted with free sack lunches and tickets to the Wild West. That afternoon the Wild West was performed exclusively for these children."

If, as the partners now began to ask themselves, the Wild West could attract such numbers and publicity and earn such handsome profits in the United States, might it not do equally well in the Old World, in Europe? They were about to find out.

CROWNED HEADS OF EUROPE

While the Wild West was clearly on a roll, both financially and artistically, it was not "one big happy family." Indeed, in the arena, some participants could get downright hostile. Though William Carver, the self-styled "Evil Spirit of the Plains," might be a fine marksman, when he got flustered, which was often, his temper flared. One afternoon, when the cowboy missed a series of targets, he broke his rifle across his horse's ears and struck an assistant.

Furthermore, Carver, Cody, and many others drank excessively. Their behavior, it was said, seriously compromised the Wild West's very existence. According to Louis S. Warren, "It was an eternal gamble, as to whether the show would exist from one day to the next, not because of a lack of money but simply through the absence of human endurance necessary to stay awake twenty hours out of twenty-four, that the birth of a new amusement enterprise might be properly celebrated."

Such problems aside, Cody and Salsbury were determined to take their extravaganza to a new level by shepherding it across the Atlantic to England. On March 31, 1887, Buffalo Bill's Wild West steamed out of New York Harbor on a chartered ship, the *State of Nebraska*. Aboard were 209 passengers, 90 of whom were Lakota

As Cody's show grew in popularity in the United States, the showman was determined to bring it overseas to display the customs and skills of the West to Europe. With his troupe of performing cowboys, sharpshooters, and American Indians and his menagerie of American animals, Cody's European tour was a success.

Sioux men, women, and children. Below deck were mules, elk, Texas steers, donkeys, a deer, 18 buffalo, and almost 200 horses. Practically everyone got seasick when, on the seventh day out, the *State of Nebraska* encountered a violent storm. With the horses suffering from poor ventilation, the ship's captain ordered holes cut in the deck to provide them with air. Several animals died and had to be thrown overboard.

On April 14, the cast sailed into the Thames Estuary, and on the sixteenth they anchored off Gravesend in Kent. British officials immediately quarantined all animals, fearing an outbreak of rinderpest and foot-and-mouth disease. The authorities, however, wanting in no way to hinder the Wild West in its journey to London, released the animals after a few days.

When it came to the ton of ammunition the production carried, there was a greater concern. Customs officers promptly confiscated thousands of bullets and, in their place, issued specially loaded blanks for arena use—except for Will Cody, Annie Oakley, and other sharpshooters who needed to use bullets in their performances.

Cody was enthusiastic about the mission before him. He told his fellow participants, as quoted in *Buffalo Bill and His Wild West*, "All of us have combined in an expedition to prove to the center of old world civilization that the vast region of the United States was finally and effectively settled by the English-speaking race." It would be this triumph of European civilization over the "savage" West, the central theme of the Wild West, that would appeal most to the new audiences eagerly awaiting Buffalo Bill.

THE OLD WEST TO THE OLD WORLD

Cody had learned that to draw the largest crowds, it was best to attach the Wild West to an existing enterprise. He had done so in New Orleans, when he piggybacked on the World's Industrial and Cotton Exposition of 1884. Cody would do something similar in London by parking his extravaganza next to the American Exhibition. That exposition, which displayed American arts, industries, manufacturers, products, and resources, would be the first of its kind outside the United States. With little faith that such an event in and by itself would attract hordes of Londoners, organizers of the American Exhibition were only too happy to "hook up" with Buffalo Bill's Wild West. Together, they believed, both enterprises would succeed.

Given its organizational efforts and the public's thirst for something as novel and exciting as the Wild West promised to be, it is doubtful, in retrospect, that Cody needed to associate with the American Exhibition. From the Royal Albert Docks in London's East End, the Wild West traveled by three trains to Earl's Court in

Kensington. Evidence of advance publicity was everywhere along the route. According to Joy S. Kasson, "Colorful posters had been slapped on every available surface for an American style media blitz that took the British press by surprise." According to Kasson, one commentator exclaimed,

> I may walk it, or 'bus it, or hansom [taxi] it: still
> I am faced by the features of Buffalo Bill.
> Every hoarding is plastered, from East-end to West,
> With his hat, coat, and countenance, lovelocks and vest.

At Kensington, hundreds of laborers erected everything from grandstands to stables. According to *Buffalo Bill and His Wild West*, "Lights and bonfires helped the workers to fence the arena, build stands, and so on. The object was to allow forty thousand people into each performance. The only hold-ups occurred when British workers could not stop staring at Buffalo Bill. He retired from view."

With plans for an extended stay, as opposed to mere one-day stands, the Wild West in London could display an array of special effects theretofore not possible. The arena was a third of a mile in circumference. Authorities spent $130,000 to construct what was to be the largest, most elaborately presented outdoor event ever. "A cadre of workers unloaded seventeen thousand carloads of rock and earth to create the simulated Rocky Mountain landscape," wrote Bobby Bridger. "Full-size trees were uprooted and brought in from the midlands to create the imaginary west of Kensington."

The swift, efficient setting up of the Wild West became a show in itself. Crowds gathered to see the expert movement of men, livestock, equipment, and wardrobe and to get a free show as performers rehearsed their various routines. As its May 9 opening day approached, Buffalo Bill's Wild West looked to be a European triumph in the making.

THE QUEEN TAKES A BOW

Key to making it so, however, would be the attraction of distinguished guests, which would generate attention-getting newspaper headlines. The first notable to comment on the up-and-coming attraction was famed British actor Henry Irving, who had seen the Wild West in New York. "You have real cowboys with bucking horses, real buffaloes, and great hordes of steers, which are lassoed and stampeded in the most realistic fashion imaginable," he declared, as quoted in *Buffalo Bill and Sitting Bull.* "Then there are real Indians who execute attacks upon coaches driven at full speed. No one can exaggerate the extreme excitement and 'go' of the whole performance."

On April 28, two weeks before the opening, former British prime minister William Gladstone appeared at the fairgrounds with a small entourage, hoping for a preview. His wish granted, Gladstone concluded that American horsemen were much better than their English counterparts.

Not to be outdone, on May 5, Edward Albert, prince of Wales (later to become King Edward VII), asked for and of course received an invitation to attend his own preview presentation. The next day, he witnessed the Wild West's first full dress rehearsal. The prince was enthralled, so much so that he couldn't wait to tell his mother, Victoria—the queen of England.

In more than a quarter of a century, the British monarch, who in 1887 was celebrating her Jubilee (50 years on the throne), had not ventured into public for any sort of entertainment. Upon hearing of Albert's glowing praise of the Wild West, however, she requested a command performance. When advised there was no way the Wild West could come to Windsor Castle, the queen consented to go to the show, at the Earl's Court arena.

Having now broken one precedent, the queen, as Don Russell noted, was ready for another.

> When the American flag was presented according to the usual Wild West custom, the Queen rose from her seat and bowed deeply and impressively toward the banner, and as her entire party joined in the salute, says Cody, "there arose such a genuine heart-stirring American yell from our company as seemed to shake the sky. It was a great event. For the first time in history, since

Word of Cody's show spread throughout London and soon government officials, celebrities, and even royalty began dropping by to preview the attractions. Edward Albert VII, then the prince of Wales, visited the show during dress rehearsal (*above*) and recommended it to his mother, Queen Victoria, who later requested a command performance.

the Declaration of Independence, a sovereign of Great
Britain had saluted the star-spangled banner, and that
banner was carried by a member of Buffalo Bill's Wild
West.

On June 20, the day before the crowned heads of Europe were
to assemble for the Queen's Jubilee at Westminster Abbey, Buffalo
Bill put on a special, abbreviated presentation of the Wild West at
Windsor Castle. Never, it seems, had so many monarchs gathered
to see a commercial show. During a simulated American Indian attack, the Wild West's Deadwood Stage carried the prince of Wales
and four kings, those of Saxony, Belgium, Greece, and Denmark.
Buffalo Bill took the reins. The prince, an avid poker player, said, as
quoted by Bobby Bridger, "Colonel, you never held four kings like
these before." "I've held four kings," said Cody, "but four kings and
the Prince of Wales makes a royal flush, such as no man ever held
before."

Two and a half million people saw the Wild West in London
during the summer of 1887. It had, indeed, taken Great Britain by
storm.

GRAND TOUR

Buffalo Bill's extravaganza was not, of course, without its critics.
When the Wild West moved on to Birmingham, in early November,
the *Birmingham Gazette* found nothing particularly remarkable
about its many acts, particularly those of American Indians. "The
Indian war cry is a decided failure," it declared. "It is apparently a
shrill and feeble screech, and not at all the blood-curdling yell that
Fenimore Cooper and other writers have led us to believe." Still, the
Gazette went on to conclude, "The show is worth seeing—it is worth
anybody's while to put himself to some trouble to go and see it."

As an aside, back in London, two performers of the Wild West,
"Bronco" Charlie Miller and Marve Beardsley, challenged two cyclists, Richard Howell and W.M. Woodside, to a six-day race at

Buffalo Bill's Wild West Extravaganza was received with enthusiasm when it debuted in Paris. Ever mindful of style and trends, local Parisians were gripped with Wild West fever and bought up all the Old West clothing and paraphernalia that was up for sale at the show.

Agricultural Hall. At the end of the first day, the cyclists, racing in their high wheelers, totaled 137 miles (220 km) and seven laps, with Buffalo Bill's pony riders at 136 miles (218 km) and six laps. The race would be run for eight hours each day, with horses being changed every hour. In the end, the cowboys won—by two miles (three km) and two laps. Miller and Beardsley had each ridden 407 miles (655 km).

In May 1888, the Wild West returned to the United States, but the following year it was back in Europe, this time to open at the

Exposition Universelle in Paris, where the Eiffel Tower had just been erected. Again, the Wild West would seek out venues where crowds were already expected to gather.

By the time the Wild West arrived in France, the shops of Paris were filled with all manner of trinkets and souvenirs, arranged for by the ever-efficient advance man, John Burke. There were toy cowboys and American Indians, saddles, ceramic buffaloes, and bucking horses as well as moccasins, blankets, and inexpensive bows and arrows. Western fashion had become the rage, with Parisians quickly adopting the style as their own.

All his success aside, traveling and performing were clearly taking their toll on Cody. "The strain of the pace he was keeping was beginning to negatively affect Cody's physical and mental health," Bobby Bridger wrote. "Today some might refer to Cody's symptoms as 'burnout,' but he was obviously suffering physically as well as mentally from the intense pressure of constant movement and performing.... Cody and all the plainsmen of his troupe were accustomed to the arid climates of the Great Plains and the Rocky Mountains, and the continual dampness of England [and the continent] kept each of them sick with colds."

With his increase in weight, due to a confused diet, plus his ever-present drinking problem, Cody, at 43, was beginning to show his age. He was burned out and homesick for the Plains. Clearly, he needed a break and a rest.

INTERNATIONAL STAR

The Wild West closed in Paris in October 1889, headed to Marseilles, France, and from there sailed for Spain. Tragically, the production arrived just when the Iberian Peninsula was experiencing a devastating influenza epidemic. Barcelona was under a partial quarantine, which obviously impacted attendance at Wild West performances. Many cast members became violently sick, with Annie Oakley nearly dying. Seven Lakota were sent home, desperately ill. In January 1890, the Wild West dragged itself out of Spain with severe losses in personnel and in dire financial straits. Cody was

Cossacks and the Wild West

Cossacks were known the world over as guerrilla adventurers, experts on horseback, and fierce fighters. They first came from the Ukrainian Steppes north of the Black Sea and the Caucasus Mountains. Of the Cossacks, the great Russian writer Alexander S. Pushkin wrote: "Always on horseback, always ready to fight, always on the alert." Cossacks of the frontier were prepared to confront an enemy at any moment. Daggers were provided even for women and children. Babies were carried in a special hood behind the back in order to leave the hands free to fight back in case of attack.

Widely known in the United States as semicivilized warriors from the Russian Empire, Cossacks were a direct challenge to the American cowboy's image of equestrian expertise and rough riding. Of them, William Cody supposedly remarked, as quoted by Louis S. Warren, "I don't know anything about Cossack riding, because I never saw any of it, but I will guarantee that our men can do anything that Cossacks can do and more, too."

To broaden its international appeal, the Wild West soon began employing Cossack riders. They performed well ... when they weren't complaining about working conditions, that is. Under the headline "WILD WEST COSSACKS STRIKE," the *New York Times* reported on May 10, 1905,

> The Russian Strike movement is spreading. The Cossacks who have been performing at Buffalo Bill's Wild West Show have struck for higher wages and have been turned by the management into the streets, where they are to be seen wandering about disconsolately.
>
> They are now anxious to resume their part in the performances, but, as they deliberately broke a contract which secured for them about five times as much as their average earnings at home, Col. Cody refuses to take them back and is already drilling another troupe of Cossacks to take their places. He is also suing the strikers for damages, and the case will be tried on Thursday.

William F. Cody, it seems, could drive a hard bargain, even when dealing with the mighty Cossacks.

getting little respite from the grinding pace of arena showmanship and production.

The Wild West arrived in Naples, Italy, on January 26, 1890. From there it was on to Rome. There, another interesting aside took place, one that again offered the kind of challenge to Wild West cowboys that simply could not be refused. The prince of Teano, Don Onorio Caetani Herzog, approached Cody, stating that he had a stable of wild Cajetan stallions that were unrideable and unbroken. No one in Italy could tame them. Would Cody, the prince wondered, take up the challenge and have his wranglers give it a try? Without hesitation, the horse-breaking bid was accepted.

John Burke once again rose to the occasion, doing all he could to promote the contest. According to Bobby Bridger, "Rumors soon flashed through Rome that the prince's stallions were so dangerous that they actually ate people. Accentuating the drama, on the day of the contest Burke had the horses brought to the arena in chains and effected special barricades to protect the crowds in the event that any of the ferocious beasts would escape. As usual, Burke's outrageous publicity antics worked; twenty-thousand Italians bought tickets to witness the event."

They probably didn't get their money's worth. Within five minutes, it was all over, with the American cowboys having all but captured, subdued, and saddled the wild horses in less time than it took to yell "yippee ki-yay."

Evidently, there wasn't all that much to the seduction. "The cowboys simply roped the wild horses, tossed them to the ground, and kept them subdued with ropes," reported Henry Blackman Sell and Victor Weybright, authors of *Buffalo Bill and the Wild West*. "Next, two cowboys on horseback rode up beside the horses as they were released and rose to their feet. Surrounded, the horses promptly learned there was no possible escape and were subdued quickly."

From Italy it was on to Germany, where the Wild West played Frankfurt, Berlin, Dresden, Bonn, Munich, and Stuttgart, among other cities. Everywhere the extravaganza went, promoting America's conquest of the West, it was a sensation. Cody had become an international star. Yet, back in the United States, trouble was brewing. The secretary of the interior, John Noble, ordered that from now on, no American Indians would be allowed permission to accompany the Wild West, wherever it went. Nobel had concluded that American Indian performers were being exploited.

AMERICAN INDIANS AND THE WILD WEST

European-Americans were, from the moment of first encounter, fascinated with Native Americans. As the *wasichus* (Sioux for "whites") pushed westward onto the Great Plains, seeking routes to the Far West or land to raise cattle and grow crops, the American Indians they encountered elicited both fear and awe. Though seen as primitive and savage (uncivilized), the Sioux, Cheyenne, and other tribes of the Plains were admired for their ability to harmonize with their surroundings, make do with what was available, and, above all, hunt and fight as the incredible centaurs that they were. In short, American Indians of the mid- to late nineteenth century were a source of never-ending curiosity, mixed with trepidation, for white immigrants seeking their "manifest destiny."

They were also in the way. As various westward trails, such as the Bozeman, the Oregon, the California, and the Mormon, opened up, immigrant encounters with warring American Indian tribes increased. The Sioux, in particular, bitterly resented the whites' intrusion onto their lands. When the United States Army, at the behest of settlers, took to building forts along the trails to protect white advancement, American Indians became even more incensed. As a result, the post–Civil War period witnessed increasing violence, perpetrated by both whites seeking what they considered land for the taking and American Indians who wanted, above all, to be left alone to continue their traditional buffalo hunting, intertribal warring, and nomadic ways.

In an attempt at peace (and subjugation), the U.S. government enticed an impressive array of Plains Indian tribes to Fort Laramie, in what is today Wyoming. The resulting Fort Laramie Treaty of 1868 sought, in effect, to buy off the Plains Indians. The treaty would give them the Great Sioux Reservation, 22 million acres (8.9 million hectares) that would later become all of the state of South Dakota west of the Missouri River, plus annuities in the form of annual payments of goods and food. In exchange, the tribes would agree to forgo attacks, not only on whites but on other tribes. Peace, it was hoped, would come to the Great Plains.

Some tribal leaders agreed to the plan and others did not. Red Cloud signed the treaty, and his bands, as well as others like them, became known as "friendlies." Other leaders like Crazy Horse and, most importantly, Sitting Bull would have none of this, and, as a result, they were forever after labeled as "hostiles." In the ensuing two dozen years, the hostiles would be hunted down by the United States Army until they were killed, driven into Canada, or subdued and brought onto reservations. By the late 1880s, "friendly" reservation Indians (Sitting Bull, reluctantly, now among them) were devastated. They were prevented from pursing their hunting lifestyles, given the worst land to exploit as yeomen farmers, and forced to begin assimilating into white culture. Many were starving, and more than a few were treated as prisoners who were thought too dangerous to be let off a reservation.

LAST CHANCE

Cody was aware, more so than most in his scouting generation, of American Indian exploitation at the hands of the U.S. government.

The Bozeman Trail

When the Montana goldfields opened up in the early 1860s, miners were desperate to find the shortest, quickest route from the Midwest to the land of riches. The Oregon Trail would get them to their destination, but it was a long, difficult, 800-mile journey. When John Bozeman and John Jacobs pioneered a new route, to be known as the Bozeman Trail, the distance to be traveled was reduced to 450 miles. In the five-year period between 1863 and 1868, when the trail was in use, more than 3,500 civilians used the wagon route to get to the gold. The military used the Bozeman Trail to travel to and from the forts it was establishing along the route.

The Bozeman Trail's shorter journey was an obvious advantage; what was less well known, however, was how dangerous the trail would become. The Sioux, Crow, Apache, and Blackfeet considered the new passage an infringement on their hunting grounds. They would oppose its use by military and civilian travelers alike.

Bozeman himself seems to have been oblivious to the fact that his road cut right through lands ceded to the Sioux. On his first trip out, in early May 1863, he and his partner were attacked by a Sioux war party that took their horses, clothes, weapons, and food, leaving them with nothing but the clothes on their backs. Undeterred, however, Bozeman, on May 27, set out at the head of a wagon train of 46 wagons and 89 men, women, and children, making it through without incident.

On December 21, 1866, a conflict between the Sioux and the U.S. Army resulted in a massacre of 80 soldiers near Fort Phil Kearny. Ironically, in the spring of 1867, Bozeman was killed by Blackfeet warriors at the Yellowstone River. The 1868 Treaty of Fort Laramie shut down the trail for good.

Though open only for five years, the Bozeman Trail had a significant effect on the region. While the Sioux won a victory in having the trail discontinued, the warfare between them and the Army that erupted in 1865–1866 signaled the start of a 10-year conflict that would see Chief Sitting Bull's tribe (and many others) all but exterminated.

As early as the 1870s, at the very time when Cody was beginning to employ American Indians in his theater productions, the frontiersman was giving voice to his feelings on the matter. "In nine times out of ten, where there is trouble between white men and Indians, it will be found that the white man is responsible," he declared, as quoted in *Buffalo Bill and the Wild West*. "Indians expect a man to keep his word. They can't understand how a man can lie. Most of them would as soon cut off a leg as tell a lie."

Yet, ironically, at the lowest point in American Indian life, when cultural survival itself was at stake, many "friendlies" chose to flock to the Wild West, to play "hostile" American Indians. They literally lined up at reservation outposts with the hope of being hired to travel with the Wild West to the East Coast and maybe to Europe. For such performers, the prospect of reasonable pay, a chance to travel, an opportunity to get away from the prying eyes of reservation authorities, and simply to interact with non-American Indian people was alluring. For some it was an alternative to imprisonment.

For Cody, of course, having American Indians on display gave his production validity. Like Buffalo Bill, American Indians were the genuine article. As Joy S. Kasson observed, "Stage actors can walk away from the parts they play, but the Wild West confounded distinctions between 'reality' and 'representation,' and just as Cody was considered a 'real' hero because of his dramatic enactments, the American Indians in his company were identified with the villainous roles they played in the show."

The distinction between image and reality was further blurred when American Indian performers, while out on tour, were also sightseers in the cities and towns they visited. Everywhere they went, American Indians were encouraged to proceed in costume. "In a Venetian gondola or a New York opera house," Kasson continued, "these men and women in blankets and feathers were a walking advertisement for the show, and the fact that they appeared the same whether on or offstage seemed to endorse the Wild West's claims to authenticity and its view of history."

Buffalo Bill's Wild West   Indianer

Cody respected American Indians and gave them a voice in his production, but because the show was designed to draw crowds of people who
knew nothing about them, these performers were forced to portray ste-
reotypes in place of real examples of American Indian lives. The images
of the American Indian in the show and popular culture quickly overshad-
owed the actual Native history and culture.

In the end, American Indians swarmed to the Wild West, re-
gardless of the demeaning roles they may have been required to play,
because it offered them the unique, last opportunity to be, even for
a short time in a play-acting way, the kind of people they had always
been—hunters and warriors of the Plains. "Offstage, the constant
movement of the Wild West from town to town, the breaking, moving and making of Cody's large camp, was the closest they [Ameri-
can Indian performers] would ever be again to their former way of
life and the Lakota nomadic tradition," Bobby Bridger observed.
"Buffalo Bill simply offered those Lakota of the horse and buffalo
culture of the nineteenth century a final chance to be themselves."

FRIENDS OF THE AMERICAN INDIAN

The Indian Rights Organization (IRO), which had formed in 1882, was not happy about what Cody was doing with the American Indians. The IRO claimed that the Wild West, and similar arena shows that had sprung up in its wake, exploited them. Having American Indians on display, whooping it up, simulating mock battles, chasing after white settlers, attacking stagecoaches, performing war dances, painting themselves from head to toe, and parading around half-naked was demeaning, and the dramatization of such savagery should be stopped, they insisted.

Furthermore, the life a performer led in show business, whether he or she is American Indian or white, was bound to be debilitating and demoralizing, the IRO claimed. "No [Indian] agent spoke in favor of Wild West shows, and the litany of evil attributed to them—syphilis, drunkenness, debauchery, rebelliousness, laziness, and just plain sin—suggest how much the convergence of Indians and show business brought America's latent antitheatricalism to the surface," wrote Louis S. Warren. The author then quoted a Kansas agent who, willingly, got to the real cause of IRO discontent: "The Indian having been educated to the 'romantic barbarism' of 'stage robbery, daring feats of horsemanship, and fantastic dressing' for centuries, 'he should now be taught useful practical lessons of real life; such as will secure him a sound body, comfortable clothing, a permanent home, and the knowledge, that by honest toil alone, men become happy, successful, and even great.'"

While the IRO, and like-minded organizations, may well have recoiled at the "evils" awaiting American Indians in the theater life, what they really objected to was the continuation of tribal traditions such a life fostered. For the IRO, it was all about assimilation, making the American Indian as white as possible, as soon as possible. "Cody's use of Indian performers, and more specifically the image he presented of them, clashed with the idealized image of the Indian championed by reformers," Sam A. Maddra wrote in *Hostiles?* "Cody presented, and indeed celebrated, the Indians as wild mounted warriors and hunters of a bygone age. The reformers 'wished to foster the ideal Indians as tamed humans in a tamed land, who were embracing civilization through land allotment, education, and industry.'"

Over and over again, the theme of assimilation came through. James McLaughlin, perhaps the most well-known American Indian agent of his time, wrote in his 1910 autobiography, *My Friend the Indian*, "To the men of my time was appointed the task of taking the raw and bleeding material which made the hostile strength of Plains Indians, of bringing that material to the mills of the white man, and of transmuting it into a manufactured product that might be absorbed by the nation without interfering with the national digestion." No wonder the IRO and various reformers sought to discredit the Wild West and restrict American Indian participation in it.

EXPLOITATION

On June 14, 1890, the steamship *Saale* landed at the port of New York carrying, among other passengers, five American Indian performers returning from Buffalo Bill's Wild West in Europe. There was Eagle Horn, Blue Rainbow, Little Lamb, Running Creek, and Kills Plenty. The assistant superintendent of immigration, James R. O'Beirne, detained the five, having concluded they were clearly in poor health. Eventually, all but Kills Plenty were allowed to proceed to their homes on the Pine Ridge Agency in South Dakota. Kills Plenty, suffering from a severely injured wrist, was unable to travel. O'Beirne had him transferred to New York's Bellevue Hospital for treatment.

The injury to Kills Plenty occurred in Germany, when a horse fell on him during a performance. The wound had been poorly treated, and soon blood poisoning set in. Kills Plenty had also contracted tuberculosis, weakening him further. The performer knew he was seriously ill, and he wished to be taken to his home on the reservation. Cody was contacted and agreed to defray any expense necessary to get Kills Plenty back to the Pine Ridge Agency. On June

18, the American Indian died—on American soil, but far from his home, family, and tribal members.

Kills Plenty was not the only American Indian performer to perish in 1890 while in the employ of Cody. On the first day of the year, Chief Hawick died of typhoid fever in Marseilles, France. Six days later, a performer named Featherman died of smallpox in the same city. On February 15, at the age of 45, Goes Flying succumbed in Naples, Italy. Then on March 2, Little Ring, just 33, died of heart disease while lying in bed.

With the death of Kills Plenty in June, the number of American Indian deaths for Buffalo Bill's Wild West tour of 1889–1890 had risen to five. While four of those died in Europe, relatively far from the prying American press, Kills Plenty succumbed in New York City, squarely in the public eye. As author Sam A. Maddra declared, "The death of Kills Plenty and the Wild West's apparent disregard for his welfare fueled the mounting opposition to Indians performing in Wild West shows."

There was more. Though it was obviously of less significance than death, critics of American Indian participation saw plenty to support their belief in the demoralizing influences outdoor show entertainment was having. No Neck, the chief of police at Buffalo Bill's Wild West, told reporters on his return to New York that he could not control his charges when they wanted to go out and "Do Paris" at night. "When I tried to do so," the chief said, as quoted in *Hostiles?*, "the braves had no ears and paid no attention."

The commissioner of Indian Affairs now threatened an investigation. For Cody, the consequences of a possible ban on further American Indian participation in the Wild West would be catastrophic. He canceled a winter tour planned for the French Riviera and arrived back in Philadelphia on November 13, determined to repudiate all charges.

CHARGES DISMISSED

The day after Cody and his entourage—Nate Salsbury, John Burke, and 38 Lakota Sioux—arrived in the United States, Salsbury, Burke,

Cody's extravaganza attracted critics along with the fans. Some people believed the show was demeaning to American Indians and encouraged people to believe that American Indians were violent savages. The American Indian performers and travelers in Cody's tour disagreed and testified that they were given fair and equal treatment. *Above,* Cody speaks with one of the American Indian performers.

and some of the American Indians headed straight to the Indian Bureau in Washington to testify about working conditions in the Wild West, while Cody went to New York. Rocky Bear was the first to be interviewed by the acting commissioner, Robert Belt, without his employers present.

"I have been in the show four years, but I think it comes out all right," Rocky Bear told Belt, as quoted in *Hostiles?* "If it did not suit me, I would not remain longer." When asked about his treatment, Rocky Bear responded, "I tell you they treated us well. If these things do not suit the Great Father, I would stop. If the Great Father do not want me to go on the show, I would go without it. . . . That is the way I get money. If a man goes to work in some other place and goes back with money, he has some for his children."

It was then Black Heart's turn to speak, to address the charges that American Indians were coerced and mistreated. "If Indian wants to work at any place and earn money, he wants to do so; white man got privilege to do the same—any kind of work that he wants," he said. Then, Black Heart went on to explain exactly why he, and his fellow American Indian performers, chose exhibition work.

> These men have got us in hand. We were raised on horse-back; that is the way we had to work. These men fur-nished us the same work we were raised to; that is the reason we want to work for these kind men. . . . What we eat was just the same as the whites eat, and we sit in the camp with them just the same, exactly. When one of our people got sick, we went for doctor; doctor looks at him. If he thinks fit to send him home, send him home right away. . . . The company have spent lots of money on us, certainly; that is what we with them for.

It was Cody's contention all along that by providing employ-ment to American Indians in his Wild West, he was, in effect, pro-moting the assimilationist cause rather than opposing it. Black Elk, who fought at the Little Big Horn and went on to write an autobiog-raphy classic, *Black Elk Speaks*, spoke eloquently to this point when he said, as quoted in *Buffalo Bill's America*, "I wanted to see the great water, the great world and the ways of the white men; this is why I wanted to go. . . . I made up my mind I was going away . . . to see the white man's ways. If the white man's ways were better, why I would like to see my people live that way."

In the end, Commissioner Belt concluded that complaints of poor treatment of American Indians in Buffalo Bill's Wild West were unfounded. "I must confess that I do not consider that any fur-ther action is required," he concluded, as quoted in *Hostiles?* Buffalo Bill could continue to hire American Indian performers.

CONGRESS
OF ROUGH RIDERS

While Nate Salsbury and John Burke were handling matters relating to supposed American Indian mistreatment in the Wild West, Cody slipped off to New York City. He didn't stay there long, however, for on the day of his arrival he was handed a telegram from General Miles, commander of the Military District of the Missouri, summoning him to Chicago. Cody hurried off, arriving there 36 hours later.

Trouble was brewing on the American Indian reservations in South Dakota, particularly at the Standing Rock Agency. Many tribes, in response to near-starvation conditions and their depression due to forced assimilation, had taken up a new religious movement known as the Ghost Dance. The faith, which required American Indian participants to dance until they fell into a trance, promised a renewal of old life ways, free from the white man's influence. As a consequence, authorities feared that "friendlies" would soon again become "hostiles" and that a major American Indian uprising was a real possibility. U.S. president Benjamin Harrison directed the secretary of war to declare martial law and assume military responsibility for suppressing any outbreak among Ghost Dancers.

Terrible living conditions and near starvation caused many American Indians to turn to a new religion called the Ghost Dance (*above*) for hope and a return to their old customs. Led by a shaman who blended American Indian and Christian beliefs, this new religion was wrongly perceived as an uprising. U.S. officials blamed Cody's friend, Sitting Bull, for organizing it.

James McLaughlin, the agent at Standing Rock, was convinced, mistakenly, that his nemesis, Sitting Bull, was behind the Ghost Dance movement and, as a result, should be arrested. If such a seizure were handled incorrectly, however, it could have triggered the very uprising everyone feared. In response, General Miles asked Cody to go to Standing Rock and, as quoted by Robert M. Utley in *The Lance and the Shield*, "Secure the person of Sitting Bull and deliver him to the nearest commanding officer of U.S. troops."

McLaughlin was not happy. Allowing Cody (a high-profile civilian) to receive credit for persuading Sitting Bull to surrender was not something the agent would accept. Therefore, when Cody arrived, officers were ordered to provide him with plenty of alcohol, to intoxicate the 44-year-old scout so he could not travel to see Sitting Bull. Nevertheless, Cody, who was famous for holding his liquor better than most, was, on November 29, 1890, off with a wagonload of gifts to arrest his friend Sitting Bull.

Cody would never make it to Sitting Bull's residence, approximately 50 miles (80 km) from Fort Yates, where the scout had arrived to begin his mission. Upon the urging of McLaughlin, Cody would be recalled by President Harrison. On December 15, with the agent's American Indian police attempting to arrest Sitting Bull, the great Hunkpapa Sioux chief was killed in an ensuing skirmish.

Sitting Bull's death (some would say murder) need not have occurred. "If they had left Cody alone," a soldier was heard to remark in the aftermath of the tragedy, as quoted in *Sitting Bull and His World*, "he'd have captured Sitting Bull with an all-day sucker." The soldier was referring to the 59-year-old chief's penchant for sweets. No one was more distraught at Sitting Bull's demise than Buffalo Bill.

THE WHITE CITY

In the spring of 1892, Cody returned to Earl's Court in London, putting on another command performance for the queen at Windsor Castle. Though the novelty of the Wild West had faded, Cody's 1892 European tour was a success. After being on the continent for almost three and a half years, however, the time seemed right to bring the grand outdoor entertainment back to the United States, where it was sorely missed.

Ever mindful of the success of setting up near a crowd-pleasing attraction, Cody hit pay dirt when his managers, John Burke and Nate Salsbury, leased a 15-acre lot across the street from the 1893 World's Columbian Exposition in Chicago. Celebrating the four-hundredth anniversary of Christopher Columbus's discovery of the New World (a year late), the fair, dubbed the "White City," would be the most successful of its kind ever. From May to October, more than 27 million people, close to half of the population of the United

When Cody decided that his show needed to return stateside, he opened up in Chicago next to the 1893 World Columbian Exposition. With approximately 27 million people in attendance, anyone who visited the exposition could not have left without at least passing Cody's production, now renamed Buffalo Bill's Wild West and Congress of Rough Riders of the World.

States at the time, attended. In one day, 716,881 took in, among other attractions, "Little Egypt" on the Midway, gondola rides, and George W. Ferris's 250-foot-diameter revolving wheel, the first to be assembled anywhere. The crowd, even to this day, may well have been the largest to ever buy tickets to a place of entertainment.

For William Cody, his now renamed Buffalo Bill's Wild West and Congress of Rough Riders of the World (to emphasize its international cast) would have its best year ever. Throngs were turned away on opening day. According to Don Russell, "The success of the exposition contributed to the success of Buffalo Bill, for no one considered that he had seen the fair unless he had also seen the Wild West." Buffalo Bill's 1893 extravaganza would see 2 million spectators and earn more than a million dollars in profit.

The Wild West's success was, in no small measure, due to John Burke's masterful publicity skills. Making the connection between Buffalo Bill and Christopher Columbus was just one example of his genius: "As Columbus was the pilot across the seas to discover a new world," the publicist declared, as quoted by Joy S. Kasson, "such heroes as Boone, Fremont, Crockett, Kit Carson, and last, but by no means least, Cody, were the guides to the new world of the mighty west, and their names will go down in history as among the few, the immortal names that were not born to die."

Furthermore, Cody's European triumphs, his success in proving he in no way sought to harm his American Indian employees, and the notoriety he gained in his attempt to secure Sitting Bull all contributed to his reputation and, by extension, that of the Wild West. Amy Leslie of the *Chicago Daily News* left a glowing portrait: "No such an engaging story-teller as Buffalo Bill figures in history or romance. He is quiet, rich in humor and mellow as a bottle of port . . . and not a dozen men I know have his splendid magnetism, keen appreciation and happy originality. He sticks to the truth mainly and is more intensely beguiling than the veriest makers of fiction."

For Buffalo Bill, 1893 was turning out to be quite a year.

THOUSAND MILE COWBOY RACE

While Cody was, of course, the star of the Wild West, its main attraction, the extravaganza, was not just Buffalo Bill. With it now being called Buffalo Bill's Wild West and Congress of Rough Riders of the World, the entertainment had evolved into a spectacle of incredible diversity. Buffalo Bill, mounted on a white stallion, would begin each performance by announcing, "Ladies and gentlemen, permit me to introduce to you the Congress of Rough Riders of the World." From that opening ovation to the final flag salute, the show offered nonstop action and excitement.

Spectators were treated to the "Grand Review," which introduced the Rough Riders and fully equipped regular soldiers of the armies of America, England, France, Germany, and Russia. "Miss Annie Oakley," the celebrated shot, then illustrated dexterity in the use of firearms. The show featured a horse race between a cowboy, a Cossack, a Mexican, an Arab, and an American Indian, on Spanish-Mexican, bronco, Russian, Indian, and Arabian horses. Races between prairie, Spanish, and American Indian girls were also staged.

"Cowboy Fun" included lassoing wild horses and riding the buckers. Spectators were also treated to the capture of the Deadwood mail coach by American Indians as well as a recreation of the *Battle of the Little Bighorn*, with scenes from Custer's Last Stand.

Folks, it seems, got their money's worth.

Some, it turned out, didn't pay at all. When Chicago mayor Carter Harrison asked World's Fair officials to admit poor children

Wild West Program

A typical *Buffalo Bill's Wild West and Congress of Rough Riders of the World Official Program* (with slight modification) looked like this:

1. OVERATURE, "Star Spangled Banner"
2. GRAND REVIEW, introducing the ROUGH RIDERS OF THE WORLD
3. MISS ANNIE OAKLEY, celebrated shot, who will illustrate her dexterity in the use of firearms
4. RACE OF RACES. Race between a Cowboy, a Cossack, a Mexican, an Arab, a Gaucho and an Indian, on Spanish-Mexican, Bronco, Russian, Indian and Arabian Horses
5. U.S. ARTILLERY DRILL, by veterans of Capt. Thorpe's Battery D, Fifth Regiment, U.S. Artillery
6. ILLUSTRATING A COW OUTFIT STARTING ON ITS ANNUAL ROUND-UP, CROSSING THE PLAINS
7. PONY EXPRESS. A former Pony Express rider will show how letters and telegrams of the Republic were distributed across our continent
8. A GROUP OF MEXICANS from Old Mexico will illustrate the use of the lasso
9. JOHNNY BAKER. Celebrated American Marksman

for free, they refused. Jack Burke, ever quick to spot a publicity coup when he saw it, declared that the Wild West would not only admit poor kids, but it would provide free transportation, candy, and ice cream. On the chosen day, 15,000 excited, delighted kids swarmed the Wild West for a treat like no other.

Then there occurred one of those asides that the Wild West was fond of picking up on, one that garnered even more publicity. Dubbed the "Thousand Mile Cowboy Race," from Chadron, Nebraska, to Chicago, it was an attempt to beat a French endurance record of 50 horseback miles (80 km) a day. The idea was to display the stamina of the western horse. The horsemen, rough riders

10. A GROUP OF RIFFIAN ARAB HORSEMEN will illustrate their style of horsemanship together with native sports and pastimes
11. LIFE-SAVING SERVICE DRILL illustrating the method of saving lives when a vessel is wrecked
12. COSSACKS, from the Caucasus of Russia, in feats of horsemanship, native dances, etc.
12. INDIAN BOY RACE
13. COWBOY FUN. Picking objects from the ground, lassoing wild horses, riding the buckers, etc.
14. INDIANS from the Sioux, Arrapahoe, Brule' and Cheyenne tribes will illustrate the Indian mode of fighting, war dances and games
15. VETERANS FROM THE SIXTH U.S. CAVALRY in military exercise and an exhibition of athletic sports and horsemanship
16. HOLD-UP OF THE DEADWOOD STAGE COACH
17. THREE MINUTES WITH THE ROUGH RIDERS OF THE WORLD
18. COL. W. F. CODY (Buffalo Bill) in his unique feats of sharpshooting while riding at full speed
19. BUFFALO HUNT
20. THE BATTLE OF TIEN-TSIN
Curtain. A Cowboy in Dodge City, 1882

all, would run for 13 days, with the average distance covered being 77 miles (123 km) a day. Each rider was allowed two horses, which were ridden alternately. Ten riders entered and five finished. A man named John Berry won the race, which ended at the entrance of the Wild West's lot.

Buffalo Bill's creation was now at the pinnacle of its power. The Wild West had, according to Bobby Bridger, "Whipped all copy-cat competitors both at home and abroad." It had become the entertainment of choice for countless Americans, providing a day's worth of incredible entertainment.

FRONTIER THESIS

As entertaining as the Wild West sought to be, it was, for Cody, always more than a show—it was also an education. The scout constantly strived for the authentic, for a true depiction of what life was like in the post–Civil War West, at least as he saw it. Yet, as the extravaganza moved into the last decade of the nineteenth century, with technological change impinging on American life (such as the light bulb, the automobile, and motion pictures and sound recording), Buffalo Bill's Wild West became something even more—a historical presentation of a vanishing era.

The 1890 census declared the frontier dead, no longer there to be conquered. The wild had become civilized. Given that reality, and the fortuitous four-hundredth anniversary of the discovery of America, it was a good time to reflect on the role of the frontier in American history. Buffalo Bill's Wild West had a great deal to say on the subject. So, too, did a 31-year-old little-known college professor named Frederick Jackson Turner.

In 1893, Turner went to Chicago to deliver an academic paper to a meeting of the American Historical Association, held in conjunction with the World's Fair. Turner was the last of five to speak to a small crowd. It is said that by the time he got up to talk, half the audience had already left. Of those who remained, half of them dozed off. Though Turner's paper, "The Significance of the Frontier in American History," attracted virtually no attention at the time it was read and published, in the coming years and decades, it would become, perhaps, the most widely discussed thesis on American history. The work made its author the most eminent historian of his generation.

Though Turner did not visit the Wild West when it was in Chicago, and Buffalo Bill did not attend Turner's lecture, the figurative meeting of both served to contrast each one's differing interpretations of what the westward movement was all about. For Cody, as depicted in the Wild West, the conquest of the West was a violent one, "of wresting the continent from the American Indian peoples, who occupied the land," as Richard White declared in *Frederick Jackson Turner and Buffalo Bill*. For Turner, the western movement was all about free land; the "essentially peaceful occupation of a largely empty continent." To Turner, the result was a unique American identity, in which Euro-Americans actually "progressed" as they went from the more civilized East to the rougher, untamed West.

For Turner, the true pioneer was the farmer; for Cody, it was the scout. To Turner, American Indians were only peripheral to his story; for Cody, they were vital. Turner believed the tools of civilization were the ax and the plow; for Cody, they were the rifle and the bullet.

While historians have long considered Turner's scholarly, academic interpretation of the westward movement legitimate, there is little doubt that the themes that Buffalo Bill's Wild West sought to articulate, through action and image, had a profound effect on how Americans at the time saw the West. Both Turner and Cody played significant roles as interpreters and facilitators of what, in their lifetimes, became a vanishing era.

BLACK AMERICA

Not all was profit and success for the Wild West—there were struggles aplenty, and the possibility of a failed season was always present. Being the biggest, most elaborate outdoor entertainment ever created, it was now costing $4,000 a day to keep the Wild West going. The pressures on Cody and Salsbury to make a profit were

Although there were plenty of African Americans working and living in the West, they were often left out of the movies, shows, and dime novels that were popular during that era. Cody, believing that he could appeal to a specific audience, organized a show depicting the history of African Americans that ultimately failed to draw crowds. *Above*, Bill Pickett stars in a rare movie about an African-American cowboy.

enormous. Cody had fainted during a couple of performances due to fatigue, and Salsbury was experiencing serious health problems. Everyone was getting older. The 1894 season would be rough for the Wild West, a considerable comedown from its peak of the year before.

Ever open to seeking new avenues for profit, Salsbury hit upon a curious idea in 1894. As an adjunct to the Wild West, he would put on a comprehensive show depicting African American life, titled *Black America*. In doing so, Cody and Salsbury went all out; no expense was spared in hiring 300 black actors, dancers, musicians, and singers. The entourage traveled from town to town in 15 railroad cars.

Why Cody chose to celebrate African Americans at this time is not clear. As Louis S. Warren was quick to point out, blacks had no story of their own in the Wild West myth. That myth was essentially in three strands. "Indians were the dispossessed noble savages who once roamed the prairies," the author declared. "Mexicans were the descendants of the first people to encounter Indians, the Spanish who fell into decadent race mixing and failed to properly conquer them. Cowboys were the vanguard of the white race that succeeded Mexicans, and finally brought progress and civilization west. There was no black component to that tripartite narrative."

Of course, in reality, blacks did just about everything whites did in the West after emancipation. They hunted buffalo, trapped beaver, cowboyed cattle, built homesteads, and fought Indians. Yet, as Warren pointed out, "Blackness was not something easily incorporated into the western story."

Cody, it is said, was no racist. Yet, in one of his autobiographies, he ridiculed black soldiers as childlike and cowardly, even though in countless instances they had distinguished themselves mightily in the Civil War. Nonetheless, Cody and Salsbury felt that if they could incorporate blacks into their show in a way that did not offend white audiences, they might draw bigger crowds.

It did not work, and it is not difficult to see why. When *Black America* opened in Ambrose Park in Brooklyn in 1895, it billed itself as a "Gigantic Exhibition of Negro Life and Character." There were displays of black people moving from savage to slave to soldier to citizen, as Warren pointed out. Slavery was seen as a necessary passage from savage to soldier. It was too much, even during the era of Jim Crow (segregation). *Black America* suffered heavy losses, and, as a consequence, so did Cody.

FAREWELL THE WILD WEST

Though the Wild West would run from 1883 to 1913, a span of 30 years, the enterprise was not Cody's only business venture. The frontiersman, having inherited his father's entrepreneurial, risk-taking sprit, still harbored the desire to establish a community or municipality out west. Though he had failed in an earlier attempt at founding the town of Rome, Kansas, in 1867, the opportunity presented itself once more in 1894 in Wyoming. This time, capitalizing on his fame as Buffalo Bill, Cody would be more successful. Wrote Stella Foote in her *Letters from "Buffalo Bill*:

> As a scout and hunter, he [Cody] had become familiar with the Big Horn Basin, the Yellowstone National Park and the surrounding majestic mountains in the heart of the Rockies. He loved the clear, blue skies, the pure air, and the refreshing smell of the pine. He enjoyed the fishing and hunting in this land where wild game was plentiful. Colonel Cody's irresistible desire to get away from the cities and into the life that was so dear to him, took him back to Wyoming, where he laid out the town of Cody in the fall of 1894. Imagine

his courage and his faith in that new country and its future!

To bring the new town, with its surrounding land development, into existence, the Shoshone Irrigation Company was formed. Cody would be its president and would put up most of the cash, and George Beck, a business acquaintance, would serve as secretary and manager. As Louis S. Warren observed, "For a better part of a decade, a river of money ran from Buffalo Bill's Wild West to the Big Horn Basin, scraping canals between river and settlers, building dams and headgates, erecting pumps, office buildings, stores, and liveries."

Cody was sure that what he was developing would become a prime tourist attraction and a fitting retirement community. "We will all have a big farm of our own that will . . . support us in our old age and we can lay under the trees and swap lies," Warren quotes Cody as announcing. The world's greatest showman would be "[w]ealthy, retired, and the revered founder of a real civilization."

Of course, there were problems in turning what was then the remote wilderness of the Big Horn Basin into a viable, accessible development. Farming the sandy sagebrush of the region was burdensome. Less than six inches of rain fell per year. The water that needed to be brought in, with the construction of 50 miles of canal digging, was high in sulfur. Attracting settlers would remain a challenge for many years to come. By the end of the nineteenth century, the population of Cody, Wyoming, was less than Buffalo Bill's Wild West traveling camp of 600.

Yet the town of Cody did survive and grow. Today, with 8,000 residents, it continues to thrive and is the home of the Buffalo Bill Museum and Historical Center.

GENEROUS TO A FAULT

William Cody was never careful with money. When he had it, he gave a great deal away to family and friends. If he didn't, literally, hand it out, he spent it on a shared good time. His wife did not care

Cody decided to establish a new settlement and chose a location in Wyoming that became available in 1894. Cody, Wyoming, was an ambitious enterprise, but the daring businessman managed to attract enough people to the area to make it thrive. The town relies heavily on tourism and holds one of the most popular rodeo competitions every year during Independence Day weekend (*above*).

for his free-spending ways. Back in 1883, when Cody had started the Wild West, Louisa (also known as Lulu) had absolutely no faith in the project. She refused to let her husband use any of the money he would send her, and she tied up every asset they owned, fearful the new enterprise would come crashing down. So incensed was Cody regarding his wife's actions—her attempt, in his eyes, to ruin him financially—that he filed for divorce. Nothing would come of the action in 1885, but 20 years later, there would be a more determined attempt at separation.

In many respects, Cody was simply an overly generous man. What he had, he shared. With the completion in 1885 of Scout's

Rest, his ranch in North Platte, Nebraska, the place became, in effect, a rest stop for friends. "On our way to North Platte, while passing the home of William F. Cody, some of the older boys said they thought Bill might be at home," recalled Frank C. Huss, as quoted in *The Lives and Legends of Buffalo Bill*. "Some 15 of us rode over to the ranch, about a mile south of the road. Cody was at home and sitting on the veranda. After hand shaking and introductions, we were asked what we would have to drink. Each called for his favorite and each was supplied. There must have been a big supply on hand!"

Cody was also a sucker for numerous get-rich-quick schemes that charlatans were only too ready to foist upon the most famous American of his time. In 1884, he joined a partnership to produce Yosemite Yarrow Cough Cream and Wonder Worker in La Crosse, Wisconsin. Later, the enterprise offered White Beaver's Cough Cream, the Great Lung Healer, at 50 cents a bottle. Next came a project, with Lieutenant Frederick Schwatka, to colonize 2.5 million acres (1 million hectares) in Mexico. In 1893, Cody and Dr. Frank Powell created Panamalt, designed as a substitute for both coffee and alcohol. The partners hoped the drink would appeal to Mormons, who drank neither liquor nor coffee. The following year, however, the Panamalt factory was forced to close, as did a livery service and hotel that Cody had opened in Sheridan, Wyoming. While William Cody did have his business successes, failures were even more plentiful.

Perhaps Cody's greatest financial debacle concerned his heavy investment in the Campo Bonito gold mine, 43 miles (69 km) from Tucson, Arizona. Gold did trickle forth from the mine, but not in sufficient quantities to make any of its investors happy. In the end, Cody would pour a half-million dollars into various Arizona mine shafts, with precious little but aggravation to show for it.

DIVORCE SUIT

Cody remained technically married to Louisa the rest of his life, but their marriage, almost from day one in 1866, was stormy and filled with difficulties. He was rugged, approachable, and western. She was elitist and reserved and preferred eastern refinements. He was a philanderer and a drinker. She was possessive and jealous. Though the two did share triumphs and tragedies with regard to business and children (of which there were four), by 1904 Cody was determined to finally terminate their relationship. In January in Cheyenne, Wyoming, he filed a petition for divorce.

The ensuing celebrity divorce trial became a national (even international) sensation, while creating a public relations disaster for Cody. "When William and Louisa Cody faced off in a courtroom, with their lawyers and witnesses, they scripted their marriage into dueling narratives, each battling for the sympathy of the judge," observed Louis S. Warren. "This was a contest in which the old storyteller and showman should have been an easy victor. But as the trial rapidly became a scandal in the mass press, it became a show of its own."

While property and money were always a contentious issue in the Cody family, the scout's case against his wife rested on two premises: one trivial, the other stunning. Cody claimed that his wife, at times, refused to let him invite friends over to their house, called Scout's Rest, in North Platte, Nebraska, where he spent his winters. When they did come, Louisa would make it so unpleasant for him that the friends were forced to leave. Cody asserted that his married life was made unbearable and intolerable under such conditions. The second complaint, the one the whole trial would turn on, was far more dramatic. Cody insisted that his wife had many times threatened to poison him.

When Cody first attempted to divorce his wife in 1885, the sudden death of the couple's young daughter, Orra, essentially halted the proceedings. Weeks after Cody filed for divorce in 1904, another daughter, Arta, also died suddenly, of "organic trouble." Louisa would claim that William's divorce petition caused such stress for Arta that she died of heartbreak. Louisa threatened to denounce her husband as Arta's murderer if he did not drop the divorce threat and permanently reconcile with her.

The actual trial didn't begin for almost a year after Arta's death. The poisoning claim by Cody rested heavily on the testimony of

Saving His Namesake

In 1875, when a group of concerned Texans asked General Philip Sheridan what might be done to stop the wholesale slaughter of buffalo, he responded, as reported in *Bury My Heart at Wounded Knee*, "Let them kill, skin, and sell until the buffalo is exterminated, as it is the only way to bring lasting peace and allow civilization to advance."

Sheridan's infamous words proved prophetic. By the early 1880s, the once mighty southern and northern buffalo herds had been all but eliminated. Cowboys and the discovery, in the early 1870s, of a method of tanning buffalo hides brought down what was at one time close to 30 million American bison.

In truth, the bison herds simply could not withstand the big commercial enterprises organized to take them out. According to *The American People: Creating a Nation and a Society, Volume II*, "Teams of one or two professional hunters, backed by a team of skinners, gun cleaners, cartridge reloaders, cooks, wranglers, blacksmiths, security guards, teamsters, and numerous horses and wagons, took to the plains. Men were even employed to recover and re-cast lead bullets taken from the carcasses."

In 1886, the Smithsonian Institution, having discovered that it had no satisfactory buffalo specimens, sent an expedition to Montana Territory in search of the animals. Luckily, they found a few wild buffalo, which they used to create a comprehensive display.

With total extinction a real possibility, it soon became clear that the 20 healthy buffalo of the Wild West could figure mightily in the survival of the species. By 1888, of the 256 buffalo in captivity, only two herds were larger than Cody's. As it turned out, Buffalo Bill's buffalo hunting reenactments in his Wild West extravaganzas actually did much to restore and save the iconic mammal of the American Plains—this from a man who claimed to have killed close to 5,000 buffalo himself. It seems that with Buffalo Bill, the ironies never cease.

Mrs. John Boyer, the wife of a ranch foreman and manager at Scout's Rest. According to Louis S. Warren, in an incident recounted at the trial by Boyer, she told how, after Louisa had said, "I will rule Cody or ruin him," she called her husband to the top of the stairs and handed him a cup of tea. "Willie, drink this it will do you good," Louisa was to have said. Cody drank the tea, lurched toward the bathroom door, and collapsed, vomiting as he stumbled. A doctor had to be called.

The poisoning accusations aside, Cody failed to convince the presiding judge that a divorce was warranted. The trial was dismissed on March 23, 1905. Cody had to pay his wife's court costs, amounting to $318.

SHERIFF AT THE GATE

Immediately after his failed divorce trail, Cody took off for Europe to tour with the Wild West. James A. Bailey, of Ringling Bros. and Barnum & Bailey Circus fame, was now managing the extravaganza, having taken over upon the death, on Christmas Eve 1902, of Cody's longtime friend and partner, Nate Salsbury. Some say Bailey booked the Wild West for an extended four-year European engagement primarily to avoid competition with his American circus operations.

When the Wild West made money, as it did for the most part during the 1902–1906 period, no one knew how to spend better than Cody. Wrote Bobby Bridger:

> When the Wild West was the world's premier entertainment attraction and making millions annually he [Cody] spent money "as if he were trying to give it away faster than he earned it." After the show Cody would go to the box office, fill his pockets with money and hit the town. The entourage of open-handed dreamers, schemers, drinkers, and beggars would begin to gather at the box office and grow as Cody stepped out into the night.

Cody bought every drink at every bar and usually drank every one under the table.

On his return to the United States in 1907, Cody, at 61, was clearly showing signs of fatigue, the strain of undertaking both management and performance duties for the Wild West. "Fluid movement of such a large body of people and livestock was a constant nightmare," Bridger observed. "Coordinating the railroad schedules alone was a full-time chore; extraordinary advance logistical planning was required to ensure that the Wild West would arrive in town on schedule, with enough time to set up its huge canvas tents, arrange and conduct a promotional parade, perform a matinee and evening show, strike the tents and move the entire operation on to the next town."

Cody was displaying clear signs of a nervous breakdown. Still, the old scout soldiered on. He simply could not afford to pull the plug on the Wild West, throwing hundreds of people, including himself, out of work.

By 1913, however, after 30 years on the road, the Wild West's time was clearly past. The show started its last tour in the South, with the weather in no mood to cooperate. For 100 straight days, the Wild West lost money. During one matinee, in good weather, it netted only $7.15.

When the Wild West reached Denver, it was attached for debts. As Cody saw the sheriff's men prowling the lot, he instructed an aide to rush to the ticket window with the hope of grabbing the day's receipts to pay off his people. The sheriff, though, got there first. Some American Indians had to sell their costumes in order to earn enough to get back home to the reservation. Cody, it would seem, was at the end of his rope, a broken man with everything behind him and no reason to meet another day.

FAREWELL TO THE WILD WEST

That, however, would not be the man anyone knew. Cody, even at 67 years of age, was anything but unemployable. He was offered $2,500 a week to star in a variety show in London. He turned down the offer, demanding twice the amount. Some wanted Cody to appear in the newly emerging entertainment medium called motion pictures. While he turned that down, too, feeling that he would, at his age, look rather ridiculous in front of the camera, the offer gave him an idea. Soon enough, the scout formed the Col. W.F. Cody Historical Pictures Co.

The concept behind the enterprise was simple; Cody would make a series of historical films depicting events in his life and the Old West. As much as possible, he would use an original cast. His first project would be a recreation of the Wounded Knee Massacre, which occurred two weeks after Sitting Bull's demise and resulted in the death of more than 300 American Indians, many of whom were women and children.

The movie was filmed on location, at the Pine Ridge Reservation, using American Indians and soldiers who had actually participated. General Nelson Miles was an adviser. The crusty old soldier insisted that, since he had commanded 11,000 troops in the field during the campaign, all 11,000 must be seen on film. Cody simply paraded the 600 troops he had available past the camera 40 times. After a few go-arounds, he closed the camera lens, and Miles was never the wiser for it. The movie, however, was a flop.

Cody next turned his attention to war, or at least the preparation for it. In 1916, with the First World War entering its second year, America was finding it more and more difficult to remain neutral in the European conflict. Cody joined a growing number of Americans who urged President Woodrow Wilson to be prepared to enter the conflict. Cody, ever the patriot, offered to create a new production, to be termed "A Pageant of Preparedness." The idea was well received, with the U.S. Army agreeing to allow Cody to recruit soldiers and obtain artillery pieces. The production would feature charging cavalry and batteries of field guns.

While all this activity kept Cody's spirits up, it drained him physically. In November 1916, he returned to Wyoming, exhausted. In December, he went to Denver. It was there that he contracted a cold. Complications set in, and Cody's wife and surviving daughter,

Having lived a long and full life, Buffalo Bill Cody died in Glenwood Springs, Colorado, in 1917. His "Wild West" legacy is commemorated at the Buffalo Bill Historical Center (*above*) in Cody, Wyoming.

Irma, were summoned. The scout recovered briefly, and on January 3, 1917, he went to Glenwood Springs, hoping its waters would benefit him. Then, on January 5, Cody suffered a nervous collapse, and he was brought back to Denver. Five days later, at 12:05 A.M., with Lulu and Irma present, the 72-year-old scout died.

Tributes poured in. Former president Theodore Roosevelt said that Cody "embodied those traits of courage, strength and self-reliant hardihood which are vital to the well-being of our nation," as quoted in *The Lives and Legends of Buffalo Bill.* When "Little Missy," Annie Oakley, was asked to write her memories of Buffalo Bill for the *Cody Enterprise*, she stated, "He was the kindest, simplest, most loyal man I ever knew."

William Frederick Cody died a poor man, but he left a rich and lasting legacy.

CHRONOLOGY

1846   William Cody is born near Le Claire, Iowa, on February 26.

1857–1859   Cody is hired as a messenger for Russell, Majors, and Waddell.

1860   Cody supposedly rides for the Pony Express.

1864   Cody enlists in the 7th Kansas Cavalry.

TIMELINE

1864: Cody enlists in the 7th Kansas Cavalry

1846: William Cody is born near Le Claire, Iowa, on February 26

1873: Cody forms the "Buffalo Bill Combination"

1866 Cody marries Louisa Frederici.

1868 The Fort Laramie Treaty establishes the Great Sioux Reservation.

1868–1872 Cody is employed as a scout.

1872 Cody guides Grand Duke Alexis of Russia on a buffalo hunt.

1873 Cody forms the "Buffalo Bill Combination."

1876 Battle of the Little Bighorn takes place on June 25; Custer is defeated.

1883 Cody presents the first Wild West show in Omaha, Nebraska.

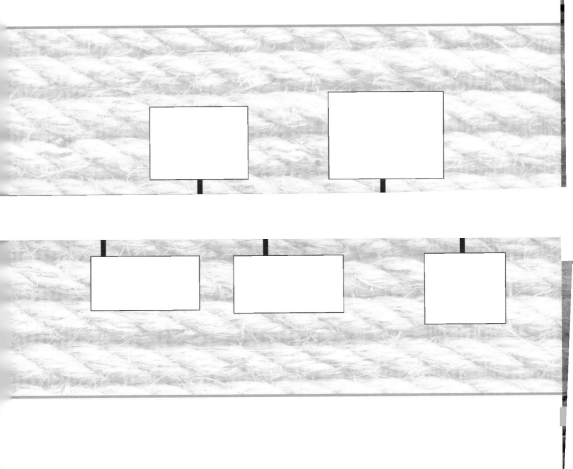

1885   Sitting Bull joins Buffalo Bill's Wild West extravaganza.

1887   The Wild West takes England by storm.

1889   The Ghost Dance begins.

1890   Sitting Bull is killed on December 15.

1893   The Wild West opens next to the Columbian Exposition.

1895–1896   Cody founds the town of Cody, Wyoming.

1905   Cody sues his wife for divorce.

1913   The Wild West is seized for debts; the Col. W.F. Cody Historical Pictures Co. is formed.

1916   Cody puts on "A Pageant of Preparedness."

1917   Cody dies in Denver, Colorado, on January 10.

GLOSSARY

abolitionist   One who favors abolishing slavery.

annuity   A sum of money or goods paid to American Indians on a regular basis.

assimilation   To absorb into a culture or mores of a population or group.

bootblack   One who shines shoes.

Bowie knife   A stout, single-edged hunting knife with part of the back edge curved concavely to a point and sharpened.

buffalo   Also know as bison; an animal with short horns, heavy forequarters, and a large muscular hump that was abundant on the Great Plains until almost exterminated in the late nineteenth century.

bullwhacker   A driver of a team of oxen.

bushwhacker   One who ambushes by attacking suddenly.

cavallard   A drove of horses or mules.

centaur   A race of creatures fabled to be half human and half horse.

clan   A division within a tribe comprising members who are usually related.

dime novel   A paperback melodramatic novel, popular in the United States from the mid-nineteenth century to the early twentieth century, usually with a western theme.

Indian   The name used to identify the aboriginal people of North America.

Indian Rights Organization   An organization formed in Philadelphia on December 15, 1882, to promote educational and civil rights for Indians.

Jayhawker   An antislavery, plundering guerrilla fighter in Kansas, Missouri, and other border states before and during the Civil War.

livery   A place for the feeding, stabling, and caring of horses.

Manifest Destiny   The nineteenth-century belief that it was inevitable that white people would control the American continent, from the East Coast to the West Coast.

messiah   A professed or accepted leader of some hope or cause.

musket   A heavy, large-caliber, muzzle-loading firearm, inferior to a rifle.

philanderer   A man who has casual or illicit sexual relations with a woman or women and, as a result, is unfaithful to his wife.

scalp   A part of the human scalp (with attached hair) cut or torn from an enemy as a token of victory.

sobriquet   A descriptive name or epithet. A nickname.

tribe   A group of individuals bound together in a permanent body, having a unified purpose. A tribe will have a common derivation, common customs, and a common language.

BIBLIOGRAPHY

"Annie Oakley: The Woman and the Legend." Squiddo. Available online. URL: http://www.squidoo.com/annieoakley.

"The Battle of the Little Bighorn, 1976." Eyewitness to History.com. Available online. URL: http://www.eyewitnesstohistory.com/custer.htm.

Bridger, Bobby. *Buffalo Bill and Sitting Bull: Inventing the Wild West.* Austin: University of Texas Press, 2002.

Brown, Dee. *Bury My Heart at Wounded Knee: An Indian History of the American West.* New York: Henry Holt and Company, 1970.

"Buffalo Bill's Wild West Show and Exhibition." Wild West Show. Available online. URL: http://www.bgsu.edu/departments/acs/1890s/buffalobill/bbwildwestshow.html.

Cody, William F. *The Adventures of Buffalo Bill.* New York: Harper & Brothers Publishers, 1904.

———. *The Life of Hon. William F. Cody, Known as Buffalo Bill, the Famous Hunter, Scout, and Guide, An Autobiography.* New York: Indian Head Books, 1991 [1879].

Corbett, Christopher. *Orphans Preferred: The Twisted Truth and Lasting Legend of the Pony Express.* New York: Broadway Books, 2003.

Croke, Bill. "The Showman of the Plains." *Range.* Available online. URL: http://www.rangemagazine.com/archives/stories/spring03/buffalo.htm.

Foote, Stella. *Letters from "Buffalo Bill."* El Segundo, Calif.: Upton & Sons, 1990.

Gibbon, Guy. *The Sioux: The Dakota and the Lakota Nations.* Malden, Mass.: Blackwell Publishing, 2003.

Gill, Jerry H. *Native American World Views: An Introduction.* Amherst, Mass.: Humanity Books, 2002.

Gray, John. *Facts Versus Fiction in the Kansas Boyhood of Buffalo Bill.* Topeka: Kansas State Historical Society, 1985.

Grey, Zane. "Zane Grey Adds the Finishing Touch to the Story by Telling of the Last Days of the Last of the Great Scouts." Buffalo Bill Cody. Available online. URL: http://www.usgennet.org/usa/topic/preservation/bios/zane.htm.

"Indian Reservations." Answers.com. Available online. URL: http://www.answers.com/topic/indian-reservation-2.

Johansen, Bruce and Roberto Maestas. *Wasichu: The Continuing Indian Wars.* New York and London: Monthly Review Press, 1979.

Kasson, Joy S. *Buffalo Bill's Wild West: Celebrity, Memory, and Popular History.* New York: Farrar, Straus and Giroux, 2000.

Kid, Kiniksu. *Buffalo Bill's Wild West.* Available online. URL: http://www.netw.com/cowboy/_feature/feature0104.html.

Larson, Erik. *The Devil in the White City: Murder, Magic, and Madness at the Fair That Changed America.* New York: Vintage Books, 2003.

Lott, Dale F. *American Bison: A Natural History.* Berkeley: University of California Press, 2002.

Maddra, Sam A. *Hostiles?: The Lakota Ghost Dance and Buffalo Bill's Wild West.* Norman: University of Oklahoma Press, 2006.

Mails, Thomas E. *The Mystic Warriors of the Plains.* Garden City, NY: Doubleday, 1972.

Majors, Alexander. *Seventy Years on the Frontier: Alexander Major's Memoirs of a Lifetime.* New York: Rand, McNally and Co., 1893.

Marshall, Joseph M. *The Day the World Ended at Little Bighorn.* New York: Penguin Books, 2007.

McLaughlin, James. *My Friend the Indian.* New York: Houghton Mifflin, 1926.

McNamara, Robert. "Dime Novel." About.com (19th Century History). Available online. URL: http://history1800s.about.com/od/1800sglossary/g/dimenoveldef.htm.

Nash, Gary and Julie Roy Jeffrey. *The American People: Creating a Nation and a Society, Volume II*. New York: Pearson, 2006.

Neihardt, John G. *Black Elk Speaks: Being the Life Story of a Holy Man of the Oglala Sioux*. New York: Simon & Schuster, 1932.

Owl, Snow. "The Great Sioux Nation." Native American People/Tribes. Available online. URL: http://www.snowwowl.com/peoplesioux.html.

"Plains Indian Timeline." Homeland. Available online URL: http://www.itvs.org/homeland/timeline.html.

"Pony Express Information." American West. Available online. URL: http://www.americanwest.com/trails/pages/ponyexpl.htm.

"The Popular Myth in Text and Image." Virginia.edu. Available online URL: http://xroads.virginia.edu/~HYPER/HNS/BUFFALO BILL/billmyth.html.

Rosa, Joseph S. and Robin May. *Buffalo Bill and His Wild West: A Pictorial Biography*: Lawrence: University Press of Kansas, 1989.

Russell, Don. *The Lives and Legends of Buffalo Bill*. Norman: University of Oklahoma Press, 1960.

Sell, Henry Blackman and Victor Weybright. *Buffalo Bill and the Wild West*. Cody, Wyo.: Buffalo Bill Historical Center, 1979.

"Sitting Bull." History by the Minute. Available online. URL: http://www.histori.ca/minutes/minute.do?id=10174.

Smith, DeCost. *Indian Experiences*. London: George Allen & Unwin, 1949.

"Soldier vs. Settler." Fort Scott National Historic Site. Available online. URL: www.nps.gov/fosc/historyculture/postofsek.htm.

Stoutenburgh, John Jr. *Dictionary of the American Indian*. New York: Random House, 1960.

"Transcript of Treaty of Fort Laramie (1868)." 100 Milestone Documents. Available online. URL: http://www.ourdocuments.gov/doc.php?flash=true&doc=42&page=transcript.

Trew, Delbert. "Indian Scouts Helped End the Indian Wars." TexasEscapes.com. Available online. URL: http://www.texas escapes.com/DelbertTrew/Indian-scouts-helped-end-the-Indian-wars.htm.

Utley, Robert M. *The Lance and the Shield: The Life and Times of Sitting Bull.* New York: Ballantine Books, 1993.

Warren, Louis S. *Buffalo Bill's America: William Cody and the Wild West Show.* New York: Random House, 2005.

Wetmore, Cody Helen and Zane Grey. *Buffalo Bill: Last of the Great Scouts.* Lincoln: University of Nebraska Press, 2003.

White, Richard. "Frederick Jackson Turner and Buffalo Bill." Study the Past. Available online. URL: http://www.studythepast.com/his378/turnerandbuffalobill.pdf.

Whittier, John Greenleaf. "Bleeding Kansas." Fort Scott National Historic Site. Available online. URL: http://www.nps.gov/fosc/historyculture/bleeding.htm.

Newspaper Articles

"Summary of Amusements." *New York Times*, November 17, 1872.

"Arrest of Buffalo Bill and Ned Buntline." *New York Times*, December 27, 1872.

"Buffalo Bill." *New York Times*, July 27, 1875.

"Buffalo Bill's Opinion of the War." *New York Times*, September 12, 1876.

"The Hostile Indian Bands." *New York Times*, September 1, 1877.

"The Trouble With the Indians." *New York Times*, September 9, 1877.

"Sitting Bull Nearly Starved." *New York Times*, November 11, 1880.

"Sitting Bull's Waning Power." *New York Times*, January 23, 1881.

"The Death of Sitting Bull." *New York Times*, December 17, 1890.

"The Wild West Show." *Birmingham Daily Post*, September 8, 1891.

Film

American Experience: Buffalo Bill, PBS Video, WGBH Educational
    Foundation, 2008.

FURTHER RESOURCES

Keenan, Jerry. *Encyclopedia of American Indian Wars 1492–1890*. New York: Norton & Company, 1999.

Kimmel, E. Cody. *In the Eye of the Storm*. New York: HarperCollins, 2003.

———. *West on the Wagon Train*. New York: HarperCollins, 2003.

Macy, Sue. *Bull's-Eye: A Photobiography of Annie Oakley*. Washington: National Geographic Children's Books, 2006.

Murdoch, David S. *North American Indians*. London: DK Children, 2005.

Penner, Lucille Recht. *Sitting Bull*. New York: Grosset & Dunlap, 1995.

Riley, Glenda. *The Life and Legacy of Annie Oakley*. Norman: University of Oklahoma Press, 2002.

Sandoz, Mari. *These Were the Sioux*. Lincoln: University of Nebraska Press, 1961.

Sayers, Isabella. *Annie Oakley and Buffalo Bill's Wild West*. Dover Publications, 1981.

Simmons, Alex and Bill McCay. *Buffalo Bill Wanted*. New York: Razorbill, 2007.

Spangenburg, Ray and Diane K. Moser. *The American Indian Experience*. New York: Facts on File, 1997.

Stevenson, Augusta. *Buffalo Bill: Frontier Daredevil*. New York: Aladdin, 1991.

Web Sites

Buffalo Bill Cody: "Who Was Buffalo Bill?"
http://www.richgros.com/Cody/who_was_he.html

An excellent Web site that offers the story of Buffalo Bill as told by various people in various ways and for various reasons. Provides an annotated listing of Web sites that present the myth of Buffalo Bill, including one on Buffalo Bill and Count Dracula.

Buffalo Bill Cody Homestead

http://www.richgros.com/Cody/who_was_he.html
A Web site that takes the viewer inside Buffalo Bill's homestead, built in 1847 by the buffalo hunter's father, Isaac Cody. The homestead is restored and furnished with items typical of the mid-nineteenth century.

Buffalo Bill Museum: Buffalo Bill—A Life in Photos

http://www.buffalobill.org/virtual_exhibits/buffalo_bill_exhibit.htm
A great set of Buffalo Bill photos, some of them quite rare. Many are available to order.

Buffalo Bill Museum & Grave: Buffalo Bill History

http://www.buffalobill.org/history.htm
A good summary of Buffalo Bill's life, along with a listing of major events and exhibits at the Buffalo Bill Museum & Grave.

Buffalo Bill's Wild West Show

http://xroads.virginia.edu/~HYPER/HNS/BuffaloBill/home.html
Excellent coverage of the buffalo hunter's Wild West show, including The Popular Myth in Text and Image, The Program, The Cast, and Chronology. Refers in particular to the 1886 show. Sponsored by ASUVA Course Projects.

William Cody (Buffalo Bill)

http://www.buffalobill.org/history.htm
A detailed biography of the famous scout, along with pictures of posters featuring the buffalo hunter.

PICTURE CREDITS

Page

9: © Infobase Publishing

15: The Art Archive/Bill Manns

21: The Art Archive

26: The Art Archive/ National Archives Washington DC

29: The Art Archive/Missouri Historical Society/Eileen Tweedy

31: Bettmann/CORBIS

40: Bettmann/CORBIS

47: The Granger Collection, New York

52: Bridgeman Art Library

57: The Granger Collection, New York

61: The Art Archive/Bill Manns

65: The Art Archive/Bill Manns

68: The Granger Collection, New York

72: The Art Archive/Bill Manns

76: The Art Archive/Buffalo Bill Historical Center, Cody, Wyoming/73.69

78: The Art Archive/Bill Manns

87: The Art Archive/Alfredo Dagli Orti

91: The Art Archive/Alfredo Dagli Orti

94: The Granger Collection, New York

96: The Art Archive/Gift of The Coe Foundation/Buffalo Bill Historical Center, Cody, Wyoming/Buffalo Bill Historical Center, Cody, Wyoming

102: Private Collection/ Courtesy of Swann Auction Galleries /The Bridgeman Art Library

107: James L. Amos/National Geographic/Getty Images

114: Danita Delimont/ Alamy

INDEX

Page numbers in *italics* indicate photos or illustrations, and page numbers followed by *m* indicate maps.

A

African Americans *102*, 103–104
Albert (prince of Wales) 75, *76*, 77
alcohol 71, 79, 95
Alexis (Grand Duke) 48–49
American Exhibition 73
American Indians
  as entertainers 63, 66–69, *68*, 77, 86–88, *87*, *91*
  exploitation of 82–92, *91*
  fighting with 18–19, 23, 25–26, *26*
  Ghost Dance and 93–95
  scouting and 39, 42–45, *45*, 55, 58
Annie Get Your Gun (Fields) 67
assimilation 88
autobiography 11–13
Avenging Angels 20, 22

B

Bailey, James A. 111
Beardsley, Marve 77–78
Beck, George 106
Belt, Robert 91–92
Bennett, Gordon II 50
Berry, John 100
birth of Buffalo Bill Cody 11, 13
bison. See Buffalo
Black America *102*, 103–104
Black Elk 92
Black Heart 92
Bleeding Kansas 14
Blue Rainbow 89
Borgia, Lucretia (gun) 37
Boyer, Mrs. John 111
boy-extras 18
Bozeman, John 85
Bozeman Trail 85
Bridger, Fort 22
Brigham (horse) 37
buffalo 36–38, 42, 48–49, 62, 110
Buffalo Bill and Sitting Bull (song) 37
Buffalo Bill Combination 54–55, 59

Buffalo Bill Historical Center 106, *114*
Buffalo Bill, the King of the Border Men (Buntline) 48, 50–51
bull-outfits 24
bull-wagon boss 24
bull-whackers 18, 24
bullying 17, 20–22
Buntline, Ned 46–54, *47*, *52*, 56
Burke, John 54, 69, 79, 81, 90, 95–97, 99
Bushwhackers 28–30, *29*, 34
Butler, Frank 64–66

C

Campbell, Gene 34
Carr (General) 42–45
Carver, William 62, 71
Chicago 53, 95–97, *96*
Civil War 28, 30–32, *31*
Cody (Col. W.F.) Historical Pictures Co. 113
Cody, Arta (daughter) 35, 38, 109–111
Cody, Irma (daughter) 115
Cody, Isaac (father) 14–16, 28
Cody, Kitty (son) 55

Cody, Louisa Frederici
  (wife) 32–36, 38, 59,
  107–111, 115
Cody, Mary (mother)
  13, 18, 23, 30
Cody, Orra (daughter)
  109
Cody, Wyoming 105–
  106, *107, 114*
coffee incident 22
Columbus, Christopher
  95, 97
Comstock, Billy
  37–38
Congress of Rough
  Riders of the World
  96–98
consumption 30, 89
Cossacks 80
Cowboy Fun 98
Crazy Horse 84
Crook, George *45*
Custer, George A. 20,
  33–35, 55
cycle racing 77–78

D

Deadwood Stage 70, 77
death of Buffalo Bill
  Cody *114*, 115
debt 112
dime novels 48, *52*, 56,
  57. See also *Specific
  titles*
divorce 107, 108–111

E

Eagle Horn 89
education 17, 23
Ellsworth, Fort 33
European tours 71–82,
  72, 76, 78, 95, 111
Exposition Universelle
  79

F

*Fact Versus Fiction in
  the Kansas Boyhood of
  Buffalo Bill* (Gray) 12
Featherman 90
Fellows, Dexter 67
Ferris wheel 96
Fields, Herbert and
  Dorothy 67
Fifth Cavalry 41–42
films 113
Fletcher, Fort 33
Fourth of July
  celebration 60–62
France 79, 90
Frederici, Louisa.
  See Cody, Louisa
  Frederici
frontier thesis 100–101
Frost, Jack 64

G

Germany 81, 89
Ghost Dance 93–95, *94*
Gladstone, William 75
Gobel, Steve 17
Goddard Brothers 37
Goes Flying 90
gold 24–25, 85, 108
Grand Review 97–98
Gray, John S. 12
Great Sioux Reservation
  84

H

Harrington, Dave
  25–27
Harrison, Benjamin
  93, 95
Harrison, Carter 98
Haslam, Bob 10–11
Hawick (Chief) 90
Hayes, Fort 35
Hays City 36

Herzog, Don Onorio
  Caetani 81
Hickok, Wild Bill 20–
  22, *21,* 32
horses 8–10, 29–30,
  33–35, 81
Howell, Richard 77–78
hunting 36–38, 48–49,
  110

I

illiteracy 13
Indian Rights
  Organization (IRO)
  88–89
influenza 79
irrigation 106
Irving, Henry 75
Italy 81, 90

J

Jacobs, John 85
Jayhawkers 28, 30–32,
  34
Jennison's Jayhawkers
  30–32
Johnston, Albert S. 20
Judson, Edward Zane
  Carroll. See Buntline,
  Ned

K

Kansas 28–30
Kansas Pacific Railroad
  33, 35–36
Kansas-Nebraska Act
  14, 34
Kearny (Phil), Fort
  18, 85
Kills Plenty 89–90
kissing affair 59

L

Lakota people 63

Laramie (Fort), Treaty of 84, 85

Laramie, Fort 22, 25, 26, 84

Leavenworth, Fort 22

legislature 51–52

The Life of the Hon. William F. Cody (Cody) 11–13

Lincoln (Abraham), Fort 55

literacy 13

Little, John 34

Little Bighorn, Battle of 33, 55, 98

M

Majors, Alexander 10–11, 12

Maleaska, the Indian Wife of the White Hunter (Stephens) 56

Marshall Field's 50

McCarthy, Frank 18

McLaughlin, James 89, 94–95

McPherson, Fort 46, 51

Medals of Honor 51

Merritt, Wesley 55, 58

Mexico 108

Miles, Nelson 93–95, 113

Miller, "Bronco" Charlie 77–78

Monarch (bison) 63

Montgomery, James 34

Mormons 20, 22, 108

Moses, Phoebe Ann. See Oakley, Annie

movies 113

mules 23, 33–35, 41

museums 106

musicals 67

N

Native Americans. See American Indians

New York 50–51, 70

No Neck 90

Noble, John 82

O

Oakley, Annie 64, 65, 67–73, 79, 97–98, 115

O'Beirne, James 89

Old Glory Blow Out 60–62

Oregon Trail 85

outfits, defined 24

P

"A Pageant of Preparedness" 113–114

Panamalt 108

Pawnee Indians 18–19

Penrose, William 42–45

Pickett, Bill *102*

Pike's Peak Express Company 8

Pine Ridge Reservation 89, 113

plays 50–54, 58, *61*

poisoning allegation 109–111

Pony Express 7–12, 9*m*

Powell, Frank 108

program, typical 98–99

Pushkin, Alexander S. 80

Q

Queen's Jubilee 77

R

railroads 33, 35–36, 70

Rain-in-the-Face 25–27, *26*

Red Cloud 84

The Red Right Hand; or Buffalo Bill's First Scalp for Custer 58

Rice, Benjamin 34

Rocky Bear 91–92

Rome, founding of 35–36, 105

Roosevelt, Theodore 115

Rose, William 35–36

Rough Riders 96–98

Royal (Colonel) 42

Running Creek 89

Russell, Major, and Waddell 12, 17, 20, 24

S

Saale 89

Salsbury, Nate 63, 90, 95

scarlet fever 55

school 17, 23

Schwatka, Frederick 108

scouting *31*, 32–35, 39–45, *40*, *45*

Scouts of the Plains 55

Scouts of the Prairie 52, 53–54

serials. See Dime novels

Seventh Kansas 30–32

Sheridan, Michael 50

Sheridan, Philip 39–42, 48, 50, 110

Shoshone Irrigation Company 106

"The Significance of the Frontier in American History" (Turner) 100–101

Simpson, Lew 20–23

Sioux 55, 58, 83–84, 85
Sitting Bull 66–69, *68*,
    84, 85, 94–95
Slade, Joseph A. 7–8
slavery 14–16, 28–30,
    29
smallpox 90
Smith, Lillian 67
Spotted Tail 48–49
spying *31*, 32
squirrels 64
stallions 81
stampedes 42
Standing Rock
    Reservation 66,
    93–95
State of Nebraska 71–72
steamships 63–64, 89
Studley, J.B. 50–51

T

Texas Jack *52*, 53

Thousand Mile Cowboy
    Race 99–100
trapping 25
Trotter, Bill 8
tuberculosis 30, 89
Turner, Frederick
    Jackson 100–101

V

Victoria (Queen of
    England) 67, 75–76

W

wagons 24, 42–44
Warbonnet Creek 55
Webb, William E. 36
Wetmore, Helen Cody
    (sister) 12–13, 33, 37
White Beaver's Cough
    Cream 108
The Wild West, Rocky
    Mountain, and Prairie

Exhibition 62–64,
    66–70
Willis, John 17–18
Wilson, Woodrow 113
Woods, George 23
Woodside, W.M. 77–78
World War I 113
World's Columbian
    Exposition 95–97, *96*
World's Industrial and
    Cotton Exposition 73
Wounded Knee
    Massacre 113

Y

Yates, Fort 95
Yellow Hand 58
Yellow River 55
Yosemite Yarrow Cough
    Cream and Wonder
    Worker 108
Young, Brigham 20, 22

ABOUT THE AUTHOR

Ronald A. Reis has written young adult biographies of Eugenie Clark, Jonas Salk, Lou Gehrig, Mickey Mantle, Ted Williams, and Sitting Bull. He is the technology department chair at Los Angeles Valley College.